The
Corporate
Lattice

Also by Cathleen Benko:

Cathleen Benko and Anne Weisberg,
Mass Career Customization:
Aligning the Workplace with Today's
Nontraditional Workforce

Achieving
High Performance
in the Changing
World of Work

The
Corporate
Lattice

Cathleen Benko

Molly Anderson

HARVARD BUSINESS REVIEW PRESS

Boston, Massachusetts

Printed in the United States of America

14 13 12 11 10   5 4 3 2 1

Library of Congress Cataloging-in-Publication Data

Benko, Cathleen, 1958-
   The corporate lattice : achieving high performance in the changing world of work / Cathleen Benko, Molly Anderson.
      p. cm.
   ISBN 978-1-4221-5516-5 (hardcover : alk. paper)   1. Organizational effectiveness.   2. Manpower planning.   3. Employee motivation.   4. Career development.   I. Anderson, Molly.   II. Title.
   HD58.9.B448 2010
   658.3'14—dc22

                                                                2010002890

The paper used in this publication meets the requirements of the American National Standard for Permanence of Paper for Publications and Documents in Libraries and Archives Z39.48-1992.

To those who create the future and arrive early.

CONTENTS

ACKNOWLEDGMENTS

Gratitude is the heart's memory.

—*B. Ellis*

A CTIONS ARE THE TRUEST MEASURE of intent. This work benefited greatly from the support of the many business leaders, researchers, academics, and professionals who opened their schedules to share their experiences and insights. Your generosity signifies the relevance of the changing world of work, and your candor added depth and rich examples of practical application. We hold you in the highest esteem.

To move from concept to action requires bold leadership. It's humbling to experience how a remarkable leadership team, led by Barry Salzberg and Sharon Allen, overturned long-held workplace beliefs and not only embraced the notion of a lattice organization, but shepherded its adoption, driving the change.

We've had the privilege of collaborating with an extraordinary community that first came together to embrace the principles and framework outlined in *Mass Career Customization*. You were the risk takers and the trailblazers, believing before the evidence. The ideas and observations of the lattice organization emerged during this collaboration, and this prequel is in many ways a tribute to your efforts.

We applaud our colleagues who contributed in so many ways. Partnership works, and the whole is surely greater than the sum of any individual's contributions. A special thank-you to Barbara Adachi, Andy Liakopoulos, and Jeff Schwartz, who profoundly influenced this effort both directly and indirectly.

Special recognition goes to our key collaborators, whose zeal, good humor, and sharp intellects inspired and sustained us:

To *Mickey Butts*—your eye for the flow of logic and skill for refining the written word is evident on every page.

To *Suzanne MacGibbon*—your doggedness in crafting, challenging, and clarifying ideas made a lasting contribution.

To *Laura Stokker*—you have the heart of a lion and have mastered both the art and science of project management. This work is stronger as a result of it.

To *Anne Weisberg*—the thesis of this book extends from our earlier works; we appreciate your contributions to all.

Thanks also to Jackie Boyle, Maggie Chao, Jennifer Clarke, Karen Crandall, and Suzanne Vickberg: you were an integral part of bringing this work to fruition. To Dave Gershenson, Suzanne Gylfe, Ken Horner, Mary McGoff, and the TEG: we appreciate the critical eye. And our thanks as well to all those who lent a helping hand, whether it was taking on more of the work of our day jobs, tracking down research studies, crafting graphics, or offering to pitch in on the home front. Your generosity fueled us.

Our heartfelt appreciation also goes to the many others, some anonymous and others not, who contributed through blog posts and other means: your views surely enhanced our thinking. Our thanks as well to our editor, Jacque Murphy, who has a knack for helping to shape our views and keep us on task.

Finally, well, there's no place like home. *From Cathy:* To George, Brendan, and Ellie, your unwavering support and personal sacrifices in support of this project, and indeed the broader base of my professional pursuits, mean the world to me. *From Molly:* To Richard, Emily, and Matthew, I am deeply grateful for your bottomless well of support and sacrifice. You are my heart and my joy, and you inspire me every day.

_____

In the spirit of Friedrich Engels, who said, "An ounce of action is worth a ton of theory," it's now time to get to work exploring ways to make sense of and respond to the change that's all around us in a concerted and deliberate fashion.

1 ▶ THE CORPORATE LATTICE

The future has already arrived.
It's just not evenly distributed yet.

—*William Gibson*

THE WORLD OF WORK is at an inflection point. The hierarchical corporate ladder is giving way to a multidimensional corporate lattice™.

Firmly rooted in the industrial age, the corporate ladder has been the prevailing paradigm for how an enterprise is organized and how it manages its work and people. At its heart, the ladder depends on an inflexible organizational worldview in which prestige, rewards, information access, and power are tied to the rung an employee occupies. Its one-size-fits-all approach assumes that employees are more alike than different. The ladder is built on a top-down, 9-to-5 notion of when, where, and how work gets done. It defines career success as a linear climb to the top.

Still today, this antiquated model shapes the ways organizations—sometimes consciously and sometimes not—operate. The mental image of a ladder is etched in our corporate consciousness and has obscured, until now, the sea change already under way.

Workplaces aren't what they used to be. Organizational structures are flatter, challenging traditional talent development models that rely primarily on upward progression. Knowledge and service work dominate the economy. Compared with traditional production processes, much of this work is less bound to a physical location. As a result of technological advances and globalization, workers are less tethered to traditional offices and set hours. And the makeup of work is changing, too. Companies use forty times as many projects now as they used twenty years ago, heightening the need for teamwork.[1] Work is changing so fast that the U.S. Department of Education estimates that 60 percent of all new jobs in the twenty-first century will require skills that only 20 percent of current employees possess.[2]

The workforce isn't what it used to be either. Family structures have changed markedly, with profound implications for a corporate ladder model predicated on a household arrangement that, by and large, no longer exists to support it. Until the 1960s, two-thirds of U.S. households were traditional, defined as Dad going to work while Mom stayed at home. That number now is down to 17 percent.[3] Women constitute half of the U.S. workforce and are the primary breadwinners for nearly 40 percent of families.[4] Men in dual-career, dual-caregiver couples now cite more work–life conflict than women do.[5]

What's more, younger generations are bringing different attitudes to work at the same time that older workers are looking for options to stay in the labor market. Almost two-thirds (70 percent) of Baby Boomers and 92 percent of Millennials (also called Generation Y) cite career–life fit as a top priority.[6] And along almost every dimension, employees are more diverse. By 2042, the U.S. workforce will be majority nonwhite.[7]

An array of similar economic, demographic, and aspirational trends is playing out in unique ways across the globe. Everywhere, a broad mix of backgrounds, interests, and needs exists among workers. Motivations vary considerably from person to person—in stark contrast to the motivations of the more homogeneous workforce for which the ladder was built.

These seismic shifts leave companies struggling to meet the challenges of the changing world of work. They signal the end of traditional assumptions about what it takes to achieve and sustain a high-performance workplace.

FROM LADDER TO LATTICE

In *Mass Career Customization*™, we provided an innovative framework to align the organization's objectives with each individual employee's goals and desire for career–life fit.[8] We also proposed a new metaphor—the corporate lattice—to characterize the changing landscape.

In mathematics, a lattice is a three-dimensional structure that extends infinitely in any direction. In the real world, lattices can be found everywhere from a garden's wooden trellis to the metalwork on the Eiffel Tower. This book delves into the power of the corporate lattice model, fully exploring its contours and applying it to real-life company practices.

In the corporate world, the lattice model organizes and advances a company's existing incremental efforts into a comprehensive, strategic response to the altered corporate landscape. It recognizes that career and life are no longer separate spheres but are now interdependent. It connects corresponding and necessary advances in talent practices with business operations to deliver both high performance and career–life fit. Figure 1-1 summarizes the key differences in beliefs and assumptions between what we call "ladder thinking" and "lattice thinking."

The shift to the corporate lattice is already going on, but as William Gibson wrote in his popular science fiction novel

FIGURE 1-1

How lattice thinking differs from ladder thinking

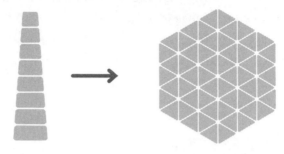

- Traditional, hierarchical structure
- Top-down authority; limited information access
- Linear, vertical career paths
- Low workforce mobility; loyalty is based on job security
- Work is a place you go to
- Individual contributor driven
- Separation of career and life
- Tasks define the job
- Many workers are similar to each other

- Flatter, often matrix structure
- Distributed authority; broad information access
- Multidirectional career paths
- High workforce mobility; loyalty is based on continuing opportunity
- Work is what you do
- Team and community driven
- Integration of career and life
- Competencies define the job
- Many workers are different from each other

Neuromancer, the future is not yet evenly distributed. Even employers who have sensed the changes have responded mostly with ad hoc, siloed, and reactive efforts that often fall short of desired results.

In essence, companies are intuitively developing corporate lattice programs—albeit through the lens of corporate ladder thinking. This book provides a metaphor to help company leaders and individuals alike visualize the shift and it offers greater clarity about the changes underway. It also describes a framework to integrate these efforts, thereby making investments already allocated more productive. It outlines the road ahead. Three core areas are central to the lattice model: how careers are built, how work gets done, and how participation in the organization is fostered (see figure 1-2).

FIGURE 1-2

The lattice organization

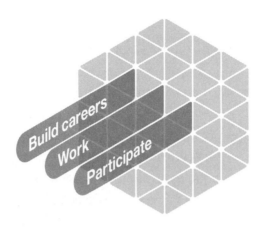

The lattice depicts employees' career paths as multidirectional, with moves across and down as well as up. The lattice metaphor does not offer a universal view of career success but rather a multiplicity of ways to get ahead—and more than one way to define what "get ahead" means. The metaphor also describes the changes in work as virtual, dynamic, and project based. Its grid resembles nodes on a network, each with the possibility of connecting "anywhere, any-time" to the others to form teams and communities. With its strong horizontal as well as diagonal and vertical supports, the visual picture of a lattice describes organizational relationships, interactions, and communication unconstrained by top-down hierarchy. Broader participation enables people to interact, get involved, share ideas, and spread knowledge throughout the company, regardless of their level on the organization chart.

The Corporate Lattice is written to help organizations see clearly the mind-set transformation taking place and to demonstrate effective ways to navigate this transformation. A handful of companies are already modeling the new thinking required to profit from the evolution from ladder to lattice. These organizations are explicitly responding to the shifts, and, in the process, they are enhancing their overall competitiveness in the talent marketplace and in the larger economy. Their successes illuminate the path ahead.

WHY LATTICE THINKING MATTERS

An implication of the changing world of work is that different things motivate different people based on a multitude of personal and professional considerations—and different things will motivate the same person at different points in his or her life. The interplay of people's unique motivations is what we term *career–life fit*. This circumstance creates a performance challenge for companies: how to *engage* members of their workforce when individuals value a career–life fit that's unique to them—and how to keep them engaged as their careers and lives change over time.

Engagement represents the extent to which employees go the extra mile to deliver extraordinary results for the company internally and to serve as brand ambassadors externally. Research has substantiated the connection between engaged employees and improved corporate operating results. One survey of thirteen thousand U.S. workers across major industrial sectors compared highly engaged employees to employees with moderate to low engagement and found that companies with highly engaged employees enjoy 13 percent higher total returns to shareholders and 26 percent higher revenues per employee.[9] Other studies have shown higher productivity, better quality, and improved earnings per share at organizations having high levels of employee engagement (see "The Power of Engagement to Drive High Performance").

Most employees, however, are not highly engaged. One study found that "only one out of every five workers is giving full discretionary effort on the job—going well above and beyond what's required because they're caught up in the passion and purpose of

The Power of Engagement to Drive High Performance

Companies with high engagement scores deliver better results than those with low scores.

- Earnings per share growth is 160 percent higher.

- Return on assets is 100 percent higher.

- Revenue growth is 150 percent higher.

- Profitability is 40 percent higher.

- Productivity is 78 percent higher.

creating a better product, service, or customer experience." Further, two out of five are "disenchanted or disengaged."[10]

Engagement is a strategic input every bit as important as capital and labor. Indeed, it is the engine of stellar individual performance that drives the extraordinary organizational performance that shareholders expect and leaders are accountable for delivering. Engagement is increasingly difficult for companies to achieve, however, because the ladder model's one-size-fits-all approach to motivating performance is ill suited to present realities.

One of the most powerful characteristics of the old workforce was its homogeneity: everyone, it was assumed, wanted the same things. But the workforce now is anything but homogeneous. Rather, a heterogeneity of backgrounds, personal circumstances, expectations, and aspirations is redefining the workplace—one with varying concepts of how work fits into life and life fits into work. The corollary is that there is no longer a single model of engagement. To achieve high performance, companies must operate amid a multitude of different ideas about success and needs for career–life fit.

The scorecard for corporate success is expanding beyond traditional measures to include engagement. Take the proliferation of rankings and awards for so-called best places to work, a recent development in corporate history. Competition is intense to earn a spot on the coveted lists, and a billion-dollar industry has emerged to help companies boost their standing. Companies display the distinctions prominently as third-party validations of their employer brand. Indeed, 88 percent use the *Fortune* 100 Best Companies to Work For icon as part of their collateral.[11]

Financial results speak just as loudly. Wharton researcher Alex Edmans found that stocks of firms on the *Fortune* 100 Best Companies to Work For list significantly outperformed market averages between 1998 and 2005, even after accounting for a range of stock market factors. Edmans concluded that "employee satisfaction is positively related to corporate performance."[12]

At least one mutual fund is putting that theory to the test: Parnassus Workplace Fund invests in companies based on their commitment to employees and the quality of their workplaces, using such lists as those published by *Fortune* and *Working Mother* as a starting point to screen firms. The fund was up more than 5 percent from inception in April 2005 to December 2009, compared with a 0.8 percent decline in the S&P 500 during the same period.[13] It has received five stars from Morningstar.[14]

The major rankings, including those from *Fortune, Business-Week, Working Mother, DiversityInc,* and the Families and Work Institute, do not rate companies strictly based on traditional ladder-oriented measures such as the generosity of compensation packages or the length of time to promotion. Instead, they gauge a wide spectrum of the drivers of engagement, including these elements:

- Pride and camaraderie

- Variety, originality, and human touch of talent programs and policies

- Learning and growth opportunities and culture

- Strength of community, collaboration, and teamwork

- Commitment to workplace flexibility

- Employees' perceptions of fairness in workplace practices and distribution of rewards

- Recognition of individual and team contributions

- Inclusiveness and diversity of leadership

- Trust and transparent communications

A common thread in the major rankings is the measurement of the drivers of employee engagement, a reflection of the motivation workers feel at the individual level. "The employee survey that the *Fortune* ranking uses is very well aligned with what we believe makes a phenomenal company: high levels of employee productivity and engagement," says Gwen McDonald, senior vice president of human resources of NetApp, the number-one ranked company on the *Fortune* 100 Best Companies to Work For list in 2009.[15] In the week after the U.S. ranking was announced, traffic to the careers section of the NetApp Web site spiked 500 percent. "It was one of our largest opportunities to build brand awareness," adds McDonald. "Customers told us, 'We love your products, but we love your people even more.'"

In short, employee engagement drives high performance. It also is a primary focus of best-places-to-work rankings, which can strengthen a company's employment brand significantly. These external rankings examine the full range of employment experience elements that diverse individuals consider important. In other words, companies are being judged by how well they recognize that engagement is no longer a static, cookie-cutter formula and the extent to which they respond by delivering individualized workplace experiences.

THE POWER OF OPTIONS

Lattice organizations provide options to customize work experiences over time, offering a multitude of ways to build careers, to work, and to participate. This strategy, in turn, benefits both the business and the individual. Just as mass product customization enables a cost-effective approach to offer customers more choices, workplace customization can be leveraged to craft cost-effective approaches to offer employees greater levels of choice, a topic we explore further in chapter 2.

Customization is compelling to employees because it gives them *option value:* the value individuals place on the ability to make choices at any point in time, and over time, whether or not they actually exercise the option. Studies show that giving employees choices about managing the "when, where, and how" of their work leads to greater job satisfaction. A recent Corporate Executive Board study found that workforce productivity rises when work–life options are available, and not merely when workers participate in such programs.[16] Individuals don't necessarily plan to exercise options to move laterally versus vertically, for example, but they feel more committed to the company because they know the option exists.

In short, employees care more about *having* options than they do about actually executing on any particular one.[17] They gain considerable comfort from knowing that alternatives are there when or if needed. Companies that give employees options are simply more likely to enjoy long relationships with them than are companies that fail to offer these choices.

The business case for moving to the corporate lattice is clear: customizing the workplace leads to a greater number of options. And with that comes option value, which boosts engagement and drives top and bottom-line results.

THE THREE WAYS OF LATTICE LIVING

To realize the value of the corporate lattice, organizations need to question unstated assumptions and overturn long-standing norms of the ladder world. *Lattice ways* describe how some companies are accomplishing this change in three core organizational areas: careers, work, and participation (see figure 1-3). Together, the three lattice ways form an integrated model that drives forward the structure, processes, systems, and culture of a company.

Next, let's explore each of these ways a lattice organization changes how it thinks and acts.

Lattice Ways to Build Careers

The ladder career model is steadily eroding. Companies are flatter, knowledge-based jobs are expanding, and the workforce has become much more mobile than in the past. The average person now holds eleven jobs in a lifetime.[18] As a consequence, rather than being a lifetime employment career destination, lattice organizations are becoming *career enhancers,* providing a range of options for the growth of marketable skills. Employees want to work for career enhancers because the skills they gain give them security in a world in which jobs change fast. Although it may be counterintuitive, the more skills and experience people are gaining, the more likely they are to stay with an employer.

Individuals are figuring out how to create lattice careers for themselves, moving in and out of companies and up and down hierarchies as their life situations change. Careers are no longer a straight climb up the corporate ladder but rather an undulating series of climbs, lateral moves, and planned descents along the corporate lattice. People can fast-track their way up the organization

FIGURE 1-3

The three lattice ways

Lattice way	Definition
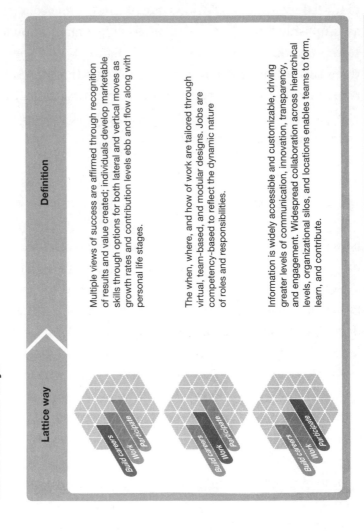 Build careers / Work / Participate	Multiple views of success are affirmed through recognition of results and value created; individuals develop marketable skills through options for both lateral and vertical moves as growth rates and contribution levels ebb and flow along with personal life stages.
Build careers / Work / Participate	The when, where, and how of work are tailored through virtual, team-based, and modular designs. Jobs are competency-based to reflect the dynamic nature of roles and responsibilities.
Build careers / Work / Participate	Information is widely accessible and customizable, driving greater levels of communication, innovation, transparency, and engagement. Widespread collaboration across hierarchical levels, organizational silos, and locations enables teams to form, learn, and contribute.

chart. They can also move laterally or develop a nonmanagement specialist role and later resume an upward climb—or not.

Demographic shifts—in particular, the evolution away from traditional family structures—are spurring demand from employees to integrate career and life. Nonlinear careers are becoming the norm. Two polls of more than 250 human resource executives revealed that two-thirds to three-quarters of respondents had made some kind of lattice-like move during their careers.[19]

The change is visible in the actions of a supervisor who devises a one-time work–life arrangement to retain a valued employee. It's seen in the side deal between a manager and an employee for a different style of compensation package—perhaps one that offers more days off rather than a salary increase. These leaders are not breaking any rules, but they're not necessarily conforming to the rules. What they're doing is not often systemic or repeatable, even though it may suffice for the moment. It's not something a company's brand can be known for, because it's not embedded into its work processes or culture.

The corporate lattice model provides a broad perspective on talent development. It moves firms from a view centered strictly on vertical progression and toward an expansive outlook centered on varied paths of customized learning and growth that are in step with individuals' career–life goals at various career stages. It formalizes opportunities for workers to progress horizontally—an acute need within flatter structures in which fewer rungs mean a smaller supply of upward moves and a need for alternative options for development (see figure 1-4). The lattice model helps organizations develop the breadth and depth of capabilities that they need to compete.

A lattice organization operationalizes career customization, making it part of the way the business runs. The finance division of a large consumer technology company showcases the changes lattice firms are making as they increase personalization, career enhancement, and career–life fit. The division has recently crafted

FIGURE 1-4

Comparison of ladder progression and varied lattice pathways

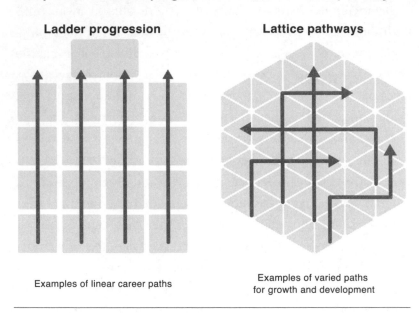

Ladder progression	Lattice pathways
Examples of linear career paths	Examples of varied paths for growth and development

a development approach that acknowledges it is a "flat organization where career development and growth opportunities occur horizontally through new learning experiences and vertically through promotions," says Betsy Rafael, vice president of finance.[20] Finance aims to build professionals who have a big-picture view of the business and can lead in outside areas. For this reason, it moves people around laterally so that they become knowledgeable about all aspects of operations. The approach also attracts, retains, and engages employees who want to be challenged professionally, something Rafael has found particularly important to many high-potential individuals.

The company's management doesn't believe there is a single talent development model that fits everyone, so it offers a high degree of customization. As one program description puts it, "Development plans are highly personalized and designed to balance the employee's skills and goals with the company's needs and initiatives." To tailor careers, the finance division provides managers and employees with several tools, including a skills assessment, a visual résumé to display an employee's portfolio of capabilities, and an individualized development plan. "To truly personalize development across the multiplicity of options the company offers, we need quality conversations between managers and employees," says Rafael. "If you adopt a personalization philosophy, dialogue is at the heart of the process. Our tools help better conversations happen."

This example demonstrates how companies and individuals are indeed migrating toward an outlook with career enhancement and customization at the core.

Lattice Ways to Work

The 9-to-5 workday in a closed-door office is becoming an increasingly rare sight in the corporate world. Knowledge and service work, which dominate the economy, are less dependent on physical location than manufacturing production work. This trend is fueled by a combination of globalization, cost cutting, and technology advances that provide radically different options for when, where, and how work gets done. Tanya Clemons, senior vice president and chief talent officer at Pfizer, sums it up this way: "In the era of the knowledge worker, it's just a totally new game now in terms of how work gets done and even what constitutes work these days."[21]

Today, more than 40 percent of U.S. employers allow staff to work remotely some of the time.[22] Employees value these opportunities to improve their career–life fit, and companies gain, too, by reducing costs and even by reducing their carbon footprint.

Moreover, many companies are sourcing talent from across the globe. To meet the demands of multiple time zones, individuals who manage global teams require flexibility in when and where they work. Teams follow the sun around the world as they sync their workdays. In line with these developments, the ratio of office space per employee is shrinking—along with associated real estate costs—as companies employ virtual "work anywhere" options.

A number of companies have notable achievements in redesigning work, but progress remains uneven. The 2008 National Study of the Changing Workforce conducted by the Families and Work Institute shows, for instance, that 87 percent of employees rate having the "flexibility to successfully manage work and personal or family life" as extremely important or very important, and yet only 50 percent of employees strongly agree that they have enough give-and-take in scheduling.[23]

Companies that do invest in improved work options to meet employee demands are finding that the company also benefits through improved performance. This is what Frontier Communications, one of the largest rural local exchange carriers in the United States, learned when it implemented a comprehensive remote work program.

While consolidating the operations of several call centers, Frontier negotiated with its union a provision that displaced call center workers could work from home. "We took a 'Let's try it and see' attitude and were very surprised with how well things worked out," says Frontier chairman and CEO Maggie Wilderotter.[24] "What was intended as a concession in a union negotiation turned out to deliver a significant productivity improvement." Indeed, 30 percent of Frontier's customer service agents now work from home, and, on average, these workers are 25 percent more productive than those who work in call centers. Retention of work-at-home agents is also 100 percent better than retention of agents who work at the center.

Along with when and where work is accomplished, how work gets done is changing, too. For instance, more work than ever before is done in free-form, boundary-crossing teams. As a consequence, companies are valuing results more than face time. They give individuals and their managers autonomy to decide how work gets done and then align performance measurements to account for this increased autonomy.

In the knowledge economy, work has become more dynamic and less repetitive and routine. Rigid, task-based job descriptions are being replaced by competency-based job definitions, along with more team-based control and decision-making over how projects get done and who is responsible for what. Cross-silo work efforts, in turn, multiply career options for employees. As Elizabeth Bryant, senior director of talent development at Southwest Airlines, explains, "We often form teams with members from several different departments. An employee might discover a new talent, or the individual might be noticed through his or her work on the team and asked to take on another role. A career path might come out of the effort."[25]

Many lattice organizations still have hierarchical organization charts, but the meaning of those charts has changed. Rather than boxes depicting rigid boundaries for an individual's scope of information access, relationships, autonomy, and power, the lattice organization's hierarchy has lines that are permeable and fluid. Matrix structures, flexible teams, and modular job designs—coupled with strategic uses of technology—enhance flexibility, speed, and adaptability.

Lattice Ways to Participate

Lattice organizations recognize that everyone can contribute—and not only within the confines of the box they occupy on the organization chart. Companies that exemplify the corporate lattice craft cultures, processes, and mechanisms that tap in to the wisdom of their workforces. They offer meaningful ways to make a difference, creating new forms of community and connection that sustain engagement and productivity.

Internet advances, known by names like Web 2.0 and social networking technologies, are radically altering the means and forms of participation. Researcher Thomas Friedman argues that the tipping point of the new "flat" world hit in 2000, when existing technologies like Web browsers, high-speed connections, and improved search engines finally reached widespread adoption, giving everyone a global platform for multiple ways of sharing knowledge and entertainment, irrespective of time, distance, geography, and, increasingly, language.[26]

Lattice ways to participate harness two interrelated forces: collaboration and transparency. Collaboration involves the flow of information and knowledge among members of teams that are formed for a common purpose. In many companies, a cross section of colleagues from different levels comes together in person and virtually to share interests, connect, create, and innovate. Technology, in turn, makes it easier to find the best people to collaborate with, and that makes working together effective, efficient, and rewarding. Location—in terms of physical proximity and position on the organization chart—has been rendered all but immaterial.

To enhance teamwork, NASA launched Spacebook, an intranet similar to Facebook and open to every employee at NASA. Spacebook features user profiles, group collaboration areas, and social bookmarking. "One of the most amazing things about these Web 2.0 technologies and the greatest value to NASA is the ability to help us create a culture of engagement and collaboration that makes each individual employee much more effective," writes Linda Cureton, chief information officer of the NASA Goddard Space Flight Center.[27] And even the ultimate in hierarchical organizations—the U.S. Army—has conducted an experiment to collaboratively rewrite seven of the field manuals that give instructions on all aspects of Army life through a wiki that every soldier can edit.[28]

A lattice organization seeks to reach the members of the workforce where they are, placing a premium on multilateral communication. It does so by proactively engaging social media technologies to provide customized communications that align with the exploding number of methods that heterogeneous workers prefer for creating, sending, and receiving information. Podcasts, blogs, text messages, tweets, wikis, webinars, avatars, and the like afford novel and memorable ways to inform workers, provide up-to-the-minute information that flows in many directions, and keep employees and external collaborators connected. For instance, Cisco chief technology officer Padma Warrior recently solicited employee thoughts, via comments on her blog and via Twitter, to gauge alignment with the company's newly announced private cloud computing strategy.[29]

Lattice organizations also instill a twenty-first-century attitude toward transparency. As technology creates unprecedented access to information, it has become easier to see into companies. Lattice organizations realize that openness protects, and even enhances, the authenticity and effectiveness of communication—a critical ingredient in increasing employee engagement and productivity and, ultimately, burnishing a company's talent brand. As communication and participation broaden, the importance of brand and reputation for individuals and organizations also rises.

Microsoft demonstrates transparency in its open-source approach to recruiting potential employees. Microsoft allows recruits to virtually experience what life at the company would be like and to make informed choices, experimenting with avatars to enable interaction.[30] Nothing is off-limits. Recruits can choose the employees they'd like to meet, the topics and questions they want answered, and the experiences in which they are interested. As they are making their decisions, prospective employees have broad access to information that typically only employees would see at other companies. In return, candidates are demonstrating to Microsoft recruiters their degree of self-motivation and interest in the company.

Examples like NASA, the U.S. Army, Cisco, and Microsoft show that the flattening of hierarchies has extended into the flattening of communication, giving people a voice and presenting organizations an opportunity for engagement. Not only does the

FIGURE 1-5

High performance and career–life fit are mutually reinforcing

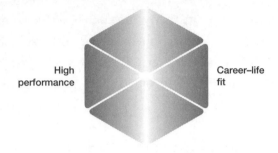

workforce's collective know-how generate ideas for measurable improvements, but it also creates an environment that is highly productive. The greater the level of collaboration and transparency, the greater the sense of belonging and the greater ownership there is in the result.

Tailor Made

Just as standardization was a key attribute of the ladder style of working, customization is a key enabler across the lattice ways to work. And the more the workplace is customized, or personalized, the more options there are for career–life fit to expand. Employees have multiple choices about ways to engage with the enterprise. Growth and development opportunities become tailored. When, where, and how work gets done grow flexible. Levels of collaboration and transparency rise, along with innovation, productivity, and efficiency.

These are among the defining characteristics of a lattice organization. Together, they deliver what companies and talent are looking for (see figure 1-5): *a high-performance culture with a sustainable career–life fit.* "High-performing companies really understand and act on the connection between high-performing people and how career and life fit together," says David Turner, executive vice president and chief financial officer of Thomson Reuters Markets. "They don't just set up policies. They actually act that way."[31]

YOUR PERSONAL GUIDE TO LATTICE LIVING

The primary purpose of this book is to help organizations see clearly the transformation taking place and to navigate the transition to the corporate lattice effectively. The next five chapters are devoted to this goal. Still, businesses are made up of individuals. Because the dramatic alteration of the workforce is a key driver of the shift toward the corporate lattice, in chapter 7 we explore the changing role each individual plays in directing his or her own lattice journey. Individuals need to treat their skills, experiences, and capabilities as valuable assets and navigate the lattice world by following three personal asset-building strategies.

- **Think option value:** Actively seek out opportunities that open up multiple future career paths.

- **Mark to market your individual assets:** Much like businesses mark their assets to market, periodically inventory your skills and experiences, assessing their relevance to the talent market and positioning them to create a consistent and compelling impression.

- **Optimize career–life fit:** Continuously seek an effective and efficient trade-off between your career and life goals at any point in time, recognizing that this is an ever-changing calculus.

Woven together, these three strategies promise that you'll experience a high level of engagement, which is linked to improved business performance. Lattice strategies for the organization and for the individual provide complementary rewards for both.

WHAT'S AHEAD

Each of these lattice ways requires a mind-set shift—a mode of thinking that is distinct from the outdated but long-lived corporate ladder worldview. Each also requires a unique approach to enhance careers, get work done, and broaden participation. But neither the thought nor the action alone is sufficient. They work in tandem. Together with high levels of customization, the three lattice ways form an integrated whole that we call the corporate lattice organization.

We have organized our tour of the lattice landscape as follows. Chapter 2, "The Changing World of Work," explains how a perfect storm of demographic and economic forces is splintering the ladder model. The need to systemically provide multiple ways to engage the diverse workforce is taking center stage, driving workplace customization as a means for companies to build a more resilient and adaptable model.

We then explore the three lattice ways, describing each and offering operational approaches and insights. Chapter 3, "Lattice Ways to Build Careers," explores how companies can redesign their talent practices through career enhancement and customization.

Chapter 4, "Lattice Ways to Work," shows how organizations can reconfigure when, where, and how work happens. Chapter 5, "Lattice Ways to Participate," examines how companies can enable broad-based, nonhierarchical forms of contribution through collaboration and transparency. As technology thinker Clay Shirky has declared, "Here comes everybody."[32]

Finally, we bring the three lattice ways together through case studies of real-life organizations and individuals. Chapter 6, "Lattice Journeys," presents case studies of Cisco, Deloitte LLP, and

Thomson Reuters finance organization, all of which exemplify how the lattice in action delivers extraordinary performance and sustainable career–life fit.

Chapter 7, "The Individual's Guide to the Shifting Landscape," concludes this book by exploring the changing role each individual plays in directing his or her own lattice journey.

THRIVING IN THE CHANGING WORLD OF WORK

Until recently, scaling the corporate ladder was the gold standard of success and the foundation on which businesses operated. But a confluence of events is leading to the demise of this century-old metaphor.

The corporate lattice is a model that organizes and structures a response to the changing world of work—elements of which are no doubt taking place within your organization. This model also has wide-ranging implications for talent practices that are proving central to a company's brand and the achievement of high performance.

Business leaders know well that, in the knowledge economy, the quality of their workforce drives the value of their shares. According to a Brookings Institution study, nearly 85 percent of a company's assets are related to knowledge and talent.[33] Companies rely on these assets to navigate—and innovate—through prosperous and tumultuous times alike.

Technology industry luminaries John Hagel III and John Seely Brown conclude, "Because talent works at every level of the corporation, the changes necessary to develop talent extend into nearly every aspect of the company's activities. Operations, organization, and strategy must all be reconceived through the talent lens."[34]

In short, the corporate lattice is a mind-set and a changed way of operating that enables companies to adapt to powerful internal and external forces. But many companies are still using corporate-ladder thinking to manage a workforce and a workplace that have shifted toward a lattice outlook. Too many companies are walking into the future backward, using the past to direct their response to the present and future. It's time to take a forward-facing stance.

2 ▶ THE CHANGING WORLD OF WORK

Change is the law of life.

—*John F. Kennedy*

THE BUSINESS LANDSCAPE CHANGES in subtle and yet profound ways. Demographic trends emerge and blend with economic shifts until, one day, the business world suddenly seems no longer recognizable with the past. A set of interlocking forces is causing the corporate lattice to take shape. This chapter describes the shifting world of work, the changes that are propelling this transformation, and the compelling benefits of becoming a corporate lattice organization.

Rather than represent only a challenge, these trends also signal an opportunity. They can be converted to a source of energy for the organization. Unlike tangible forms of power, however, the source takes the form of employee engagement. As businesses tap this wellspring—with an approach customized to the unique view of success each individual holds—employees are motivated to deliver high performance.

THE ENGAGEMENT FACTOR

Engagement describes the extent to which employees are motivated to perform at a high level and to advocate for their company's products and services externally to neighbors, relatives, or friends, for example. Numerous studies have documented the quantifiable benefits of engagement. Companies with high engagement scores boast the following.

- **Improved shareholder value:** Firms with top-quartile employee engagement realized 2.6 times the earnings-per-share growth as firms with below-average engagement.[1] Over a five-year period, companies with highly engaged employees also generated 13 percent greater total shareholder return than companies with less-engaged employees.[2]

- **Higher return on assets:** Companies in the top quartile of employee engagement experienced double the return on assets of those in the lowest quartile.[3]

- **Higher revenue growth:** Companies in the top quartile of employee engagement had 2.5 times the revenue growth of companies in the lowest quartile.[4]

- **Higher quality:** Health care facilities with engagement scores in the top 50 percent had medication error rates as much as 25 percent lower than facilities with engagement scores in the bottom half.[5]

- **Higher profitability and productivity:** Asian companies with high engagement scores were 40 percent more profitable and 78 percent more productive than those with low scores.[6]

TABLE 2-1

Service sector dominates developed economies

Percentage of gross domestic product by sector

Country	Agriculture %	Industry %	Services %
United States	1.2	19.6	79.2
United Kingdom	0.9	22.8	76.2
France	2.2	20.3	77.4
Germany	0.9	30.1	69.0
Japan	1.4	26.4	72.1

Source: Central Intelligence Agency, The World Factbook (Washington, DC: CIA, 2008).

The strategic importance of engagement is due in part to basic economics. Some 70 to 80 percent of work in many of the largest developed economies is now classified as services and knowledge work rather than agriculture or manufacturing, as shown in table 2-1.

Given the nature of service and knowledge work—"service with a smile," a creative ad campaign, or a scientific breakthrough—high performance largely depends on the degree of commitment that workers *feel*. As a result, it is becoming commonplace for corporate performance dashboards to monitor and hold business leaders accountable for engagement scores.

The problem is that even though many corporations have worked diligently to seize the opportunity these results promise, few have achieved the level of engagement they seek. As you saw in chapter 1, few employees are fully engaged, and nearly half are disengaged. The economic downturn that began in 2007 brought engagement even lower; the engagement of the highest performers fell 25 percent in 2009 alone, at a time when companies could least afford a decline in individual commitment.[7] To be sure, the engagement code is proving difficult to crack. An array of trends has brought about so many changes that to engage today's workers—and unlock the economic value of that engagement—companies need to move decisively toward the corporate lattice model.

FORCES OF CHANGE

The corporate ladder model was designed for a world of work that largely no longer exists. It is no wonder engagement is difficult to achieve.

In every aspect, employees are now heterogeneous. There is no longer an abundant supply of interchangeable workers who can be mixed and matched for optimal efficiency. Different things motivate different people at different points in their lives. And thanks to equally significant dislocations inside organizations, these diverse employees build careers, work, and participate in rapidly multiplying ways.

Seven powerful, interrelated forces are changing the world of work (see figure 2-1).

- Nontraditional families with nontraditional needs make up most of the working population.

- Women's and men's workplace needs and expectations are increasingly similar.

- Flattened organizational structures have eliminated many avenues for traditional advancement.

- The skills gap is continuing as companies have critical skilled jobs that they cannot find educated and experienced workers to fill.

FIGURE 2-1

The forces driving the changing world of work

Rise in nontraditional families

Converging expectations of women and men

Flattened hierarchies

Shortage of critical talent

Evolving needs of generations

Virtual, connected workplace

Multicultural workforce

Changing world of work

- Across generations, employees want more career–life options.

- Technology is expanding the ways work gets done.

- Workers are more multicultural than ever before.

We examine next the forces of change one by one, exploring how, in aggregate, they are altering business as we know it.

The Rise in Nontraditional Families

In the 1950s, nearly two-thirds of family households in the United States had one spouse in the workforce (usually the husband) and one staying at home (usually the wife). Work received a man's full attention in most families, and the home front generally had the woman's full attention. Few spouses juggled significant responsibilities at both work and home.

Now, only about one in six families fit this traditional mold. Instead, the vast majority is composed of parents who both work, single parents, or other family permutations (see figure 2-2). One consequence is that mothers are now primary breadwinners or "co-breadwinners" in more than 65 percent of American families, according to the groundbreaking 2009 Shriver report. The report argues that this fact "fundamentally changes how we all work and

FIGURE 2-2

Nontraditional families are now the norm

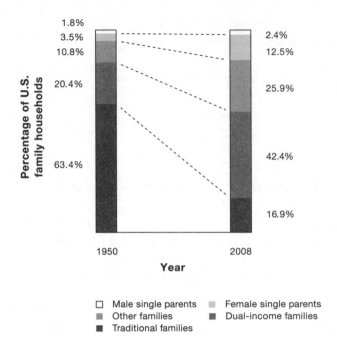

Year

☐ Male single parents   ▨ Female single parents
■ Other families   ■ Dual-income families
■ Traditional families

Source: Catalyst, *Two Careers, One Marriage: Making It Work in the Workplace* (New York: Catalyst, 1998). With updated data for 2008 from U.S. Census Bureau, *America's Families and Living Arrangements: 2008* (Washington, DC: GPO, 2009).

live, not just women but also their families, their co-workers, their bosses, and their communities."[8]

In these contemporary family arrangements, people's work lives and home lives have become like a multivariable equation with multiple constraints. Families must juggle competing work schedules and often must cope with several school and child care drop-off and pickup times, after-school activities, and the usual household chores that the stay-at-home spouse previously handled. Single-parent and blended households often manage the schedules of multiple children and adults, in a wide variety of living situations, each with different school calendars, commitments, and activities.

Elder care is also a rising responsibility facing families of all kinds. In 2007, nearly 25 percent of U.S. households cared for older relatives, and that number is expected to jump to 40 percent over the next two decades.[9] The cost to U.S. businesses from lost productivity of employees caring for elderly family members is already more than $33 billion per year.[10]

The same pattern holds true around the world. China faces a widening array of family types, many of which are quite recent in the nation's history, including single parents, dual-income families with no kids, people who are single by choice, cohabitating couples, and second marriages.[11] Patterns are also changing in India, where workers have traditionally relied on extended families to care for children and older parents. Nuclear families are now on the rise, as are assisted living centers.[12]

The global wave of evolving household configurations is chipping away at the base of the corporate ladder, whose model is predicated on a family structure that by and large no longer exists. Consider the H1N1 flu pandemic that spread around the world in 2009. U.S. president Barack Obama urged parents to keep their kids home from school if they were sick, but he also acknowledged the domino effect this would cause for working parents and for employers trying to get work done. Who would stay home, and who would cover at work? The lines between work and life have blurred, and in the process the corporate ladder has weakened.

The Converging Expectations of Women and Men

Women's numerical importance within companies has increased dramatically since they began working outside the home in significant numbers starting in the 1970s. The 2008 National Study of Employers found that, among employers with one thousand or more employees, more than half have greater numbers of women than men.[13] And for the first time in U.S. history, women now make up about half the working population overall.[14] Globally,

1.2 billion women worked outside the home in 2007, nearly 20 percent more than a decade earlier.[15]

The number of women who work outside the home is directly related to their rate of higher education. In the United States, women earn 58 percent of all bachelor's degrees and 60 percent of master's degrees, and those numbers are estimated to keep rising gradually through 2016.[16] In Europe, women constitute 55 percent of college graduates.[17] The trend extends far beyond Western countries: in Iran, for example, almost 60 percent of college students are women.[18]

As more women have entered the workforce, the expectations of women and men have changed. With education and increased workforce participation, women have developed high career aspirations. For the first time, women's goals do not differ significantly from men's: for U.S. workers under age twenty-nine, there is no gender difference in their desire for jobs with more responsibility.[19] Not only do young women say they want the same responsibilities as do young men, but young women with children do not feel differently from those who have no children.[20]

Although women are a vital part of organizations, their careers often play out differently from those of men. Many women are not employed continuously throughout their working years: one study of MBA graduates found that ten or more years after graduation, four in ten women had taken a career break, but only one in ten men had done so.[21]

For a long time, the dual roles of career woman and household manager have made it hard for many women to fit into the traditional corporate ladder model of success. But gender roles are combining as women become a greater part of the workforce and as more men want the same things as women. Of families with kids, 70 percent have a working mother, and that changes men's roles at home and affects what they need at work. "Men's and women's views about appropriate work and family roles have converged," declares the 2008 National Study of the Changing Workforce.[22]

FIGURE 2-3

Men are reporting more work–life conflict than women

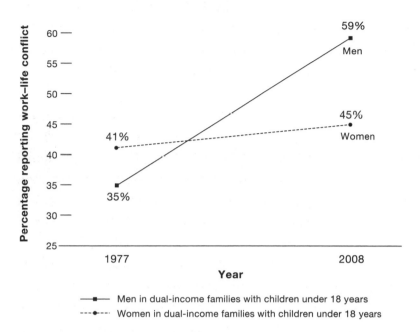

Source: Families and Work Institute, *Nation's Study of the Changing Workforce 2008*; US Department of Labor, *Quality of Employment Survey*, 1977.

Three-quarters of married working men now live in dual-income households, whereas in 1977 about half did, and men now are much more involved in child care and household duties than in the past.[23] Over the past thirty years, the amount of time men spend on child care has tripled, and time spent on housework has doubled.[24] American men are not alone in spending more time on "family work." Between 1965 and 2003, men in twenty industrialized countries increased their share of shopping, housework, and child care from less than one-fifth to more than one-third.[25]

Significantly, men now report much more work–life conflict than women (see figure 2-3). In a 2006 U.S. study of men and women in medium- and large-size companies, 31 percent of professional men, compared with 18 percent of professional women, cited work–life balance as less than satisfactory.[26] Men, too, want options for integrating career and family, but these are "most often misperceived as 'women's issues' in Washington and statehouses around the nation," argues Michael Kimmel, a sociology professor at Stony Brook University who has written several books on men and masculinity.[27]

A sign of men's dissatisfaction with how their work and life fit together is shown in CareerBuilder.com's annual surveys of working fathers between 2004 and 2009. Far from the traditional image of men who prefer work to family duties, the surveys indicate that as many as half of these men would leave their jobs if their wives' compensation were high enough.[28] Against the backdrop of financial uncertainty, the figures declined in 2009, but 31 percent would still quit, and about the same percentage would trade lower pay for additional time with their children.[29]

So women and men want to contribute, but they need much more flexibility from their companies in return. Across the genders, the corporate ladder model is splintering.

Flattened Hierarchies

Undetected over the past few decades, the foundation beneath the corporate ladder has been shifting. The ladder is built on the top-down management structure of the modern corporation, which evolved throughout the twentieth century in response to the increasing size and complexity of industrial operations. By the mid-1950s, for example, General Electric had defined levels that were planned ten years in advance.[30]

But elaborate hierarchies are a thing of the past. In recent decades, organization charts have flattened considerably. For example, GE had seventeen layers in 1980 but only seven by the mid-1990s.[31] In the United States, the number of corporate division heads who report directly to the CEO has increased 200 percent, while the levels in the management hierarchy between division heads and CEOs have declined 25 percent.[32] The typical span of control in a company is now estimated to be between fifteen and twenty subordinates per manager. In the past, the number was six direct reports per manager.[33]

Behind the flattening is global competition, which has relentlessly pressured businesses to improve performance across a number of dimensions, among them the ability to adapt. As Thomas Friedman noted in *The World Is Flat*, it has felt as if the size of the world has shrunk, first from medium to small and then from small to tiny.[34] Companies have also become more efficient—a necessity as globalization has brought competition from low-cost players. Business process reengineering in the 1980s and 1990s was emblematic of investments to reinvent the organization by streamlining processes, leveraging technology, consolidating or eliminating previously discrete tasks, and rationalizing the layers of management needed. Management studies highlighted fewer layers as a key to performance. One analysis in the early 1990s pointed out that lackluster U.S. auto companies had seventeen to twenty-two layers, whereas Toyota had only seven.[35]

At the same time, the evolution from an economy based on manufacturing to one based on knowledge and services has contributed to making rigid hierarchies—which were developed to support the fixed nature of mass production—less relevant. In 1972, manufacturing companies accounted for 70 percent of the one hundred largest employers in the United States, United Kingdom, France, Germany, and Japan. By 2002, manufacturing's share had dropped to 30 percent.[36] "Since the 1990s, Australian businesses have been moving away from management hierarchies that contain several layers of management through which a talented professional could be promoted," says Ray Glennon, director of professional services at SHL Group, a global provider of talent management and assessment tools. "The corporate ladder has become redundant. Vertical promotions are now less frequent and management positions more demanding."[37]

As hierarchies have shrunk, opportunities to climb the ladder have also shriveled. This development has called into question one of the core value propositions of the corporate ladder: that *up* is the path to success.

Few firms have done much to evolve their operating practices and cultures to make them less reliant on upward progression to motivate people. Even executives who think of themselves as enlightened must back up their words with actions. The CEO of a high-flying technology company that prides itself on its lattice structure and achievement culture, for example, publicly announces promotions to employees but doesn't make similar announce-ments about employees' significant achievements in their current positions. What's really being valued at this company?

The Shortage of Critical Talent

Nations around the world face an acute shortage of skilled workers, even during recessionary times, because of the growing gap between the supply of educated workers and the demand for their services.

The economic downturn that began in 2007 put this mismatch into sharp focus: U.S. unemployment rates for people with college degrees were half that of the overall unemployment rate.[38] Despite average unemployment of more than 10 percent in the fall of 2009, unfilled jobs remained in critical sectors such as health care, accounting, and government because employers could not find applicants with the right qualifications.[39] The issue isn't confined to a single country: a 2009 Manpower survey found that 30 per-cent of companies around the world reported having difficulty fill-ing open positions owing to shortages of people with key skills.[40] These shortfalls become more acute during an economic recovery.

Companies are concerned about not only the qualifications of new workers but also the capabilities of existing employees. More than one-third of companies say their employees' skills are not aligned with current priorities. In one global survey of companies, more than half reported that "the inability to rapidly develop skills is the primary workforce challenge."[41]

Many countries are also failing to create a long-term pipeline of workers having the education required to participate in the knowledge economy. China will need seventy-five thousand business leaders by 2017, for instance, but only an estimated three thousand to five thousand people with the required leadership skills were available in 2007.[42]

The skills gap is a problem in the United States as well. The U.S. Department of Education estimates that 60 percent of all new jobs in the early twenty-first century will require skills that only 20 percent of the current workforce possesses.[43] By almost every measure, the U.S. educational system is failing to create those skills, leading to sizable gaps in both academic achievement and high-school completion between the United States and higher-performing countries. "The persistence of these educational achievement gaps imposes on the U.S. the economic equivalent of a permanent national recession," states a 2009 McKinsey report.[44] The report adds, "The recurring annual economic cost of the international achievement gap is substantially larger than the deep recession the U.S. is currently experiencing."

Indeed, the U.S. gross domestic product would have been as much as $2.3 trillion higher in 2008 had the United States succeeded in closing the international achievement gap prominently identified twenty-five years earlier, the report concludes. That equals a 16 percent premium over current U.S. GDP. Clearly, the skills and achievement gaps are costly problems.

In addition, the aging of the population in much of the developed world will produce a wave of retirements among older, experienced workers. Between 2000 and 2010, 24 million older workers in the United States, almost one-fifth of experienced employees, stopped working.[45] Of the 80 million Baby Boomers (those born between 1946 and 1964), half of those aged sixty-two are now moving into retirement. Generation X, right behind the Boomers (born between 1965 and the late 1970s), is little more than half the size of the Boomer generation. This demographic will create a shortage of middle and senior managers until those born between the late 1970s and the mid-1990s—Generation Y— mature.[46]

The growth rate of the working-age population is slowing in many countries. The next four decades promise a much lower workforce growth rate than the prior four decades, as shown in figure 2-4. Some countries, such as Japan and Germany, project negative rates; in other words, their workforces will contract.[47] Economic growth creates new jobs, but there will be relatively fewer new workers to fill them. The European Union, for example, faces a projected shortfall of 20 million workers in 2030.[48]

Simply put, there will not be enough qualified people to do the important work that needs to be done in the years ahead. While government and some businesses are investing in education, the investments will take many years to bear fruit. In the meantime, an aging workforce coupled with growing gaps in global skills and achievement mean that companies will have to compete fiercely for top workers for years to come. And they will need to fight over the dwindling supply of critical talent using strategies far different from those of the past.

The Evolving Needs of Generations

Three generations, each distinct in its attitudes and beliefs, are interacting in the workplace. Generational differences—and similarities—among Millennials (also known as Gen Yers,) Gen Xers, and Baby Boomers are having a profound impact.

FIGURE 2-4

Growth of the working-age population is decreasing across major economies

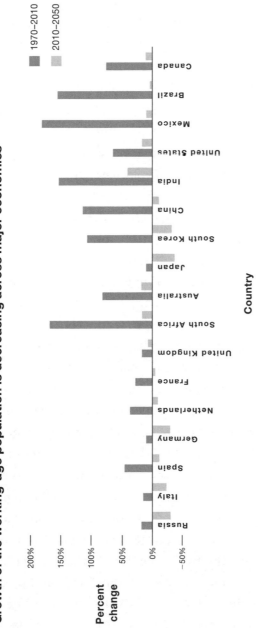

Source: United Nations, Department of Economic and Social Affairs, Population Division, *World Population Prospects: The 2008 Revision.* New York, 2009.
http://esa.us.org/unpp

The enormous Baby Boomer generation, for example, is reaching retirement age, but a significant number of its members do not want to stop working completely. Many Boomers want more options for staying engaged in work than existed in the past, and still others need to work longer than they expected because of the steep decline in the value of their retirement savings.

Tamara J. Erickson's book *Retire Retirement* encourages Boomers to redefine their notions of careers and success by tapping in to their "hunger for renewal."[49] According to the AARP—which no longer uses its full name, because the term *retired persons* does not fit its 40 million members—"Rapidly growing numbers of people over 50 are thinking of retirement not as a time to quit work entirely but as a chance to switch to work that better suits them and is more fulfilling."[50]

Boomers and Generations X and Y are more alike than different in their desire to fit life and work together: 13 percent of workers in Generations X and Y, compared with 22 percent of Baby Boomers, say they consistently put work over family.[51]

But the younger generations also have a different set of expectations. A survey taken in late 2008 of U.S. Generation Y professionals working in *Fortune* 500 companies found that even though 69 percent said they were satisfied at work, 48 percent said they planned to stay at their current employers two years or less.[52]

Moreover, Generation Y thinks about employment differently and is motivated less by money and more by meaningful work and a chance to contribute. Consider Andrew Canter and Craig Segall, two Stanford Law School students who started a campaign to change the way law firms work. In a general letter to law firms published online, the two wrote, "We recognize that changes in work structures come with an economic cost, and we are willing to be paid less in exchange for a better working life."[53] Gen Y workers also place a premium on how their work is designed. "We get stifled when we're offered single-dimensional jobs," says Justin Pfister, founder of Open Yard, an online retailer of sports equipment. "We are multidimensional people living and working in a multidimensional world."[54]

Each generation may want unique types of job choices, in part because it is in a separate life stage from the others. For Baby Boomers, sabbaticals or the chance to mentor younger workers may be attractive, whereas Generation Xers may value more the ability to work from home or access stretch assignments that give them new experiences, although sabbaticals may be attractive as well. Millennials may not care where you send them, as long as they have rich learning experiences and set their own hours. Understanding these differences is vital.

The Virtual, Connected Workplace

Thanks to inexpensive, pervasive, high-speed communication technologies, more work can be done anywhere at any time. The cost of moving data across a broadband network has dropped 90 percent in ten years, and data storage costs per unit fell from more than $500 to just over 10 cents during the same period. Computing power, measured in costs per one million transistors, also became much cheaper, dropping from $222 in 1992 to $0.27 in 2008.[55] Dramatic price declines have contributed to significant increases in Internet access. Almost three-quarters of North Americans are active on the Internet, and more than half the population in Europe and Australia are Internet users as well. Access is lower in Latin America, Asia, and Africa but growing at high rates.[56]

In the past, employees had to clock in to work at a fixed place and time. Many employees still do. But thanks to ubiquitous and fast connections, the confines of distance and physical presence are steadily weakening.

Now, going to work can well mean walking to your home office and joining a videoconference with team members around the globe. In the United States, more than 13 million people, or about 9 percent of employees, work outside a traditional office space almost every day, and another 10 million telecommute at least one day per week.[57] Worldwide, the number of workers who work remotely is projected to increase from 760 million in 2006 to 1 billion in 2011.[58] And an "office" no longer means an assigned, fixed location but rather is shorthand for the place, virtual or physical, where an individual's work is done at any given time.

Customer service operations have been early adopters of this new way of working. For instance, Mary Driffill is a reservations agent for JetBlue Airways in Salt Lake City. All the company's fifteen hundred agents work from home; collectively they handle more than thirty thousand calls each day.[59] Driffill works out of her four-year-old daughter's bedroom "under the watchful eye of Raggedy Ann, Potbelly Bear, and Gracie's other dolls, and occasionally, Chewy, a Pomeranian-Chihuahua mix," according to a *Fast Company* article.[60]

The part-time, work-from-home arrangement eliminates the need for an expensive centralized call center at JetBlue offices and increases loyalty among the many at-home moms and dads who work the phones. They appreciate the flexible schedule in a field known for high turnover. When call volume is down, an operations manager offers voluntary time off to the first agents who respond. To make this model work, good communication is essential. Managers hold monthly in-person training sessions and staff meetings, and they gather everyone for a family day each year.[61] John Nader, a JetBlue call-center supervisor, contacts the twenty-two agents on his team every few days by phone or e-mail.[62] In the corporate lattice world, management by walking around has been replaced with management by calling around.

The workday has also been extended in the corporate lattice environment, morphing from 9 to 5 to whatever works for the global team. Workers in New York, for example, may break for dinner before participating in conference calls well into the evening with colleagues in Mumbai. They may agree to check e-mail and take phone calls at night and on weekends in exchange for the flexibility to control their schedules.

Each of these work arrangements is substantially different from those that were popular in the days of the corporate ladder. Not only must organizations establish new expectations about how work gets done, but many must also adapt to a workplace in which the traditional private office is an endangered species and where the former signs of success—the size, location, and even furniture and decor in an office—no longer apply.

In addition to providing many more options for when, where, and how work gets done, Web 2.0 and social technologies like Twitter, Facebook, and Second Life are opening up unique means of collaborating, sharing information, and getting to know people across teams and locations. The office watercooler can now refer to either a physical appliance or a virtual stream of online chatter. Facebook had topped 350 million users by December 2009—250 million of them gained in only the preceding seventeen months—and Twitter had a growth rate of more than 1,000 percent from mid-2008 to mid-2009, making it the fastest-growing social media site.[63] Meanwhile, wikis, blogs, and discussion forums offer many ways to tap in to the wisdom of the crowd. There's now a multiplying universe of round-the-clock workplaces that operate as a blend of physical and virtual work.

The Multicultural Workforce

One of the greatest differences between the corporations in which younger and older workers grew up is the level of diversity, particularly in race, ethnicity, nationality, and culture. The upshot is that in a more diverse environment, one-size-fits-all workforce programs designed for a more homogeneous past are a poor fit for many people.

Among the most significant changes in the United States is the notion of what "minority" means. In 1960, the United States was 10 percent nonwhite. As we approach the 2010 census, that number is estimated to be 34 percent.[64] The U.S. Census Bureau calculates that by 2042, Americans who identify themselves as Hispanic, black, Asian, American Indian, Native Hawaiian, and Pacific Islander will together make up 54 percent of the population, a transformation that is taking place faster than researchers anticipated only a few years ago. The percentages of Hispanics and Asians alone will nearly double within the next forty years.[65] Whites are already becoming the minority in many U.S. counties and states.[66] And the number of people who identify themselves as multiracial is growing at a faster rate than any other racial or ethnic group, changing the notions of how people self-identify and are perceived.[67]

Employees who simultaneously participate in multiple cultures and identities have trouble checking a single box to describe themselves. Such changes in perception widen the range of options for participation and connection that groups seek as well as increase the countervailing desire to work in companies that recognize and relate to workers as individuals.

Another factor in the growing diversity of the U.S. workforce is the influx of foreigners, whose numbers are projected to rise to more than 2 million a year by 2050.[68] Significantly higher birthrates among immigrants are a primary reason the racial, ethnic, and cultural makeup of the U.S. labor pool is becoming more diverse faster than predicted a few years ago. In many developed countries, immigrants are sustaining the workforce, particularly as the population ages. In Canada, for example, 70 percent of the net growth in workers comes from immigration.[69]

People who have different racial, ethnic, and cultural identities often hold different values about work. Groups tend to have varied needs for flexibility because of everything from cultural expectations to the prevalence of nontraditional family types, and this variety of needs can make it harder for organizations that don't focus on work–life issues to be successful in recruiting and retaining some people of color.

Companies require multiple ways to engage with people who are different from each other as well as multiple ways to get diverse people to work together constructively. Workplace programs in the past assumed that people were more similar than different, and that led them to target efforts to the common denominator: white males with spouses who stayed at home. But worldwide, only 17 percent of educated workers are white males, with women and people of color constituting the remainder.[70] And with many companies participating in the global marketplace and often hiring labor offshore, people of widely varying cultures and nationalities must learn to work well together as never before.

Notwithstanding increasing diversity among the working population, however, many organizations have yet to achieve or capitalize on that diversity. Despite significant investments and leaders' public commitments to attract, retain, and advance diverse people, companies struggle to make strong headway toward the goal of a diverse workforce, as evidenced by the very small numbers of people of color in middle management and higher positions. Organizations have yet to harness the measurable bottom-line returns that come from having a variety of people working together to solve problems.

ENGAGEMENT IS IN THE EYE OF THE BEHOLDER

Taken together, these trends reflect a changing world of work, with a significant implication: in the lattice world, there is no longer a single model of engagement. What motivates individuals is as varied as the diverse backgrounds, cultures, family structures, and experiences that come together at work. And what "success" means differs from one individual to another, and changes as people move through various life circumstances. Employee engagement is no longer a static formula. Given this reality, cookie-cutter ladder approaches will not be as effective as they were in the past.

The move from one to many engagement models is driving a parallel trend toward *customization* of the workplace. Individual choice is becoming central to achieving employee engagement and gaining its associated business benefits. Lattice organizations are therefore hardwiring customization into the ways they operate. They are personalizing workplace practices so that they can cost-efficiently provide opportunities that each individual values.

The approach is inspired by mass product customization, which affordably engages a wide variety of consumers. Adopted in the 1990s, MPC has enabled companies to tailor everything from a double vanilla latte (hold the foam) to jeans that fit your measurements to individually designed financial products.[71] Businesses can now cost-effectively produce offerings to meet millions of individual consumer preferences. As figure 2-5 illustrates, between the 1970s and 1990s, product variety proliferated in everything from cable channels and sports shoes to car models and television screens. MPC strengthens brands as it draws customers into a closer connection, increasing satisfaction and differentiating one company from others.[72]

For example, GAO—the Government Accountability Office—the investigative arm of Congress, has crafted a unique mentoring program that individuals can tailor based on their needs and career level. It includes written resources, career courses, group mentoring, individual mentoring, and facilitated discussions of issues identified by staff. "We have benchmarked our program against other organizations, and I believe ours really stands out because it's not a one-size-fits-all. It has a variety of approaches," explains Cynthia Heckmann, GAO's former chief human capital officer. "I think that's the key. It's flexible, so it meets a lot of different kinds of needs."[73]

By applying customization to talent processes and programs, lattice companies offer multiple models to engage people and derive benefits similar to those seen with mass product customization, as shown in table 2-2. When employers customize their workplaces, they give employees choices about things that engage them, such

FIGURE 2-5

Consumer options are exploding

Percent increase in U.S. product varieties

■ Early 1970s
▨ Late 1990s

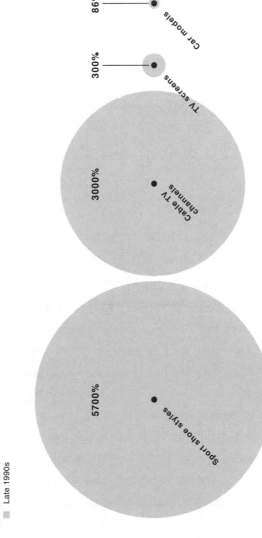

86% Car models

300% TV screens

3000% Cable TV channels

5700% Sport shoe styles

Source: Fabrizio Salvador, Manus Rungtusanatham, Anil Akpinar, and Cipriano Forza, "Strategic capabilities for mass customization: Theoretical synthesis and empirical evidence," *Academy of Management Proceedings,* 2008, р. 7.

TABLE 2-2

Shared benefits of mass customization

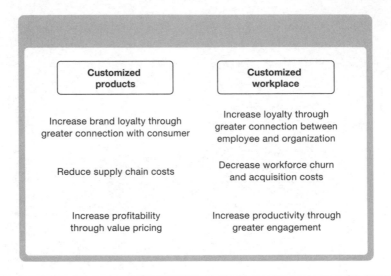

Customized products	Customized workplace
Increase brand loyalty through greater connection with consumer	Increase loyalty through greater connection between employee and organization
Reduce supply chain costs	Decrease workforce churn and acquisition costs
Increase profitability through value pricing	Increase productivity through greater engagement

as the times when and the places where they work, the benefits they can select, and the growth and developmental experiences they'll receive. Customization creates a more personalized work experience than the ladder model provides. The more people feel they have a say in the decisions that affect their experience, the more connected they feel to the organization, and the more "worth it" they believe it is to work hard to produce high performance.[74] The result is greater levels of retention, loyalty, and engagement and ultimately stronger relative financial performance.

Customization provides a means for employers to respond with multiple ways to engage today's diverse workforce. "I've seen a significant shift over the past decade among my workforce," says Mary Petrovich, CEO of AxleTech International, a $530 million supplier of off-highway and specialty-vehicle equipment components. "Previously, salary was the primary driver of job satisfaction, while today it is a blend of being fairly compensated for meaningful work at a sustainable pace."[75] People look to piece together such individualized elements as purpose, rewards, recognition, and accelerated growth and development, for example, and then mesh them with their own need for family time, personal pursuits, health and fitness, and community involvement.

One Gen Y blogger points out that he and his peers think of success in terms of both career *and* life rather than either/or. "My purpose is to be successful, genuinely happy, and to make a difference in this world somewhere along the way," he says. "Not a single one of these values can take a backseat to another. I don't want to choose. I want a blended life." There's a blurring of the line between career and life, and this blurring is itself a force driving the move toward multiple models of engagement. This writer continues: "My home time is not sacred. I have grown up being connected 24 hours a day. I have no problem with sending a quick work e-mail or organizing my in-box during these supposed 'off' hours."[76]

Jill is a midcareer new mom who also refuses to allow old definitions to confine her, but she finds it isn't easy: "For me, career success occurs when I am challenged and feel that I make valuable contributions to the organization *and* when I also feel successful at balancing the other priorities in my life. I've had many roles and in all I have felt challenged and felt the ability to contribute, but I haven't always felt successful."[77]

A variety of things will engage people and make them feel successful at the individual stages of their careers and their lives. Parents of young children tend to value flexibility highly, for example, whereas those later in their careers often place a greater premium on opportunities for new challenges. Whatever it is that drives employees, lattice organizations offer a spectrum of options to personalize work and at the same time meet the needs of the business.

Customization is the enabler of a lattice organization. It gives structure, scale, and efficiency to an organization's efforts to engage individuals of all kinds amid the changing world of work.

The workplace and the workforce have been irreversibly altered. The corporate ladder that supported work for more than a hundred years, with its singular view of success and one-size-fits-all approach, must also evolve. Engagement drives outstanding financial and operational results, but it is simultaneously more difficult to achieve when leaders fail to understand and tap in to the power of individualized workplace experiences.

Lattice organizations understand how to achieve high performance in this changing world of work. To engage a diverse workforce, they make it possible for their employees to tailor aspects of career and life. As you will learn in the chapters that follow, the corporate lattice model offers customized options to build careers, to work, and to participate. It offers a response that's not only personalized but also systemic and scalable.

3 ▶ LATTICE WAYS TO BUILD CAREERS

Success is not a place at which one arrives, but rather the spirit with which one undertakes and continues the journey.

—*Alex Noble*

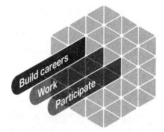

PERSONAL VIEWS OF SUCCESS are bringing the cookie-cutter career to an end. Employees with diverse goals and experiences are moving up, across, and even down the organization chart—sometimes in collaboration with their employers, and sometimes not. Their goal: a custom-tailored career that fits them.

"There are more permutations of success than we used to have," says Mike Davis, senior vice president of global human resources at General Mills, a $15 billion consumer products company. "Every function used to have narrow jobs with narrow progression structures. You do this job, then you do that job, then you do one of only two jobs. Everybody was down the center of the fairway. Now we're seeing much more mixing and matching—cross-functional assignments, cross-country assignments, people taking time off for personal leaves and then coming back. It's really quite varied."[1]

The once sacrosanct ladder career model is too inflexible to engage employees across all these variations. For nearly a century, the ubiquitous corporate ladder depended on a shared understanding that each rung was a relatively fixed destination that most people were motivated to attain. Employee development focused on this shared goal. Success meant a steady ascent, generally with the same employer and often for the length of a person's career. Without expressly saying it, companies were, in effect, *career destinations*—places where employees stayed for a long while. In return, people counted on a secure job and a comfortable retirement. In the ladder model, the better a career destination a company became, the more people wanted to work there.

The changing world of work, however, is dismantling the corporate ladder step by step. Tom Peters, best-selling author of *In Search of Excellence,* sums it up this way: "It's over. No more vertical. No more ladder. That's not the way careers work anymore. Linearity is out. A career is now a checkerboard. Or even a maze. It's full of moves that go sideways, forward, slide on the diagonal, even go backward when that makes sense. (It often does.) A career is a portfolio of projects that teach you new skills, gain you new expertise, develop new capabilities, grow your colleague set, and constantly reinvent you as a brand."[2]

THE NEW CAREER LANDSCAPE

The workplace is experiencing a "careerquake"—a "shaking of the foundations of traditional conceptions but with the opportunity to build new and more robust structures in its wake"—says A. G. Watts, professor of career development at the University of Derby

TABLE 3-1

A comparison of ladder and lattice thinking about careers

Ladder career norms	Lattice career norms
Low rates of job mobility	High rates of job mobility
Uniform career–life needs	Varied career–life needs
Linear careers with vertical climbs in lockstep progression	Nonlinear careers with lateral and vertical moves that vary over time
Few acceptable ways to alter career paths	Multiple acceptable ways to contribute and succeed
Promotion a key measure of success	Growth and development a key measure of success
Lifetime jobs with "career destination" employers prized	Continual, customized development with "career enhancer" employers valued

in the United Kingdom.[3] Concepts like "protean," "boundary-less," and "kaleidoscope" careers are emblematic of the ferment in the field with respect to the decline of company-defined career paths and the rise of new motivations for career growth.[4]

Such ideas speak to what we see as multiple realities altering long-held expectations and assumptions about how careers are built (see table 3-1). These changing expectations and assumptions share an important underlying insight. Employees are most engaged in their work when continual growth and development fit the various stages of their lives.

For one thing, people are switching jobs much more frequently than before, creating a new definition of loyalty. "Loyalty as a function of time is a dated idea," says Jaerid Rossi, process engineer at Specialty Minerals. "Work is only appealing if there is constant learning."[5] Career enhancement, with its options-based approach to development, is a powerful tactic for responding to increased job mobility and ensuring a flow of talent into and through an organization.

At the same time, fitting career and life together—what we call career–life fit—is more important to more people than ever before. Even in a period of high unemployment, a 2009 Corporate Executive Board study found that the importance of work–life balance is second only to compensation in attracting new employees to an organization.[6] The finding held true for both genders; some 56 percent of men and 58 percent of women said it is critical. Among the under-thirty crowd, work–life balance is the most important factor when deciding whether to join or remain at an employer, even more important than growth in compensation or skills.[7]

As people move through the stages of their lives, their particular models of success play out as a range of choices about how to navigate work and life. In combination, these choices, in large part, have given rise to nonlinear careers.

In this chapter, we take a look at zigzag careers and explore the opportunity side of the careerquake. Customization, in fact, enables an effective response to all the variations going on. We demonstrate two applications that are integral aspects of an enhanced career architecture: lattice pathways and career customization. Together, they broaden what's possible for individuals and companies alike.

Career Enhancement Is the New Career Advancement

The days of lifetime employment have faded away. Job mobility has increased dramatically in recent decades. Men's job tenure best illustrates the change, because men have been in the labor force longer than women. Economics professor Henry S. Faber of Princeton University has found that from 1973 to 2006, men's job tenure declined a sharp 25 percent.[8] Men are also much less likely now to have a position that lasts more than ten years. Faber concludes that "the nature of the private-sector employment relationship in the United States has changed substantially in ways that make jobs less secure and workers more mobile. What is clear is that young workers today should not look forward to the same type of career with one firm experienced by their parents."

The shift away from lifetime employment is also evident in the ways that saving for retirement began to change in the late 1970s. Before that point, companies and workers assumed long-term employment, and thus companies offered pension plans as the crown jewel of benefits. Then came the Revenue Act of 1978, which introduced 401(k) plans. By 1982, major corporations like Johnson & Johnson, JC Penney, Honeywell, and Hughes Aircraft Company had rolled out 401(k)s.[9] The plans were intended to control costs, but by being portable across employers they also chipped away at the foundations of lifetime employment. In 2009, pension plans covered a mere 21 percent of U.S. employees.[10] In effect, the barriers to exit are low for workers, and that contributes to increased mobility.

To be sure, ladder as well as lattice companies foster talent development and provide advancement opportunities. But lattice organizations think differently: they recognize that continual growth needs to be market relevant to retain and engage people in the absence of lifetime job security; instead they focus on being *career enhancers*. Career enhancement has, in effect, replaced career advancement as the ideal for employees and employers alike.

To some leaders, providing employees with career-enhancing growth experiences that make them more marketable might seem counterintuitive: why would a firm devote resources to developing skills that employees may take elsewhere? But developing these skills is what makes people *stay* and motivates them to go the extra mile. People mentally sign up with their employers every day, in effect deciding whether to stay and how much effort to give. This is in stark contrast to the occasional mental reviews of job satisfaction that happened during long-term ladder tenures. Yes, companies will lose some people in whom they've invested.

But the larger payoff is in commitment and productivity. When employees keep their skills current in the process, it helps both the individual and the company be more competitive. And companies can use the help. For example, a Corporate Executive Board study in 2009 calculated that only about one in five leaders in company succession pools is ready for the next role—a significant concern for organizations.[11]

Individuals realize they must keep their skills honed and do not hesitate to move—sometimes within the company and sometimes elsewhere—if they are not getting opportunities to stay relevant and marketable. Work experiences that offer learning are highly valued, and, in return, employees are consistently engaged, striving to excel in all that they do.

A number of recent studies have shown the premium that employees place on career-enhancing growth and development.

- Two-thirds of MBA graduates in a 2008 Aspen Institute study identified "challenging and diverse job responsibilities" as the most important criterion in choosing which job offer to accept. Stretch assignments are the currency that talent prefers.[12]

- Three-quarters of employees are looking for a change, and almost half of individuals who want a new job cite a desire for better growth.[13]

- Roughly one-third of workers quit in the first six months, and more than 60 percent of them leave because they are disappointed with growth opportunities.[14] From the start, individuals are evaluating their prospects for development.

Younger workers, in particular, understand the high probability that they will work for significantly more employers over the course of their careers than did preceding generations. In particular, Millennials stand out for their belief in continuous growth and development. Job-hopping is one technique some members of this generation employ to supercharge their growth.[15] "Gen Y knows that there are no lifetime jobs anymore and we're each responsible for our own careers," writes Penelope Trunk, author of *Brazen Careerist* and founder of the company and blog of the same name. "The best way to keep yourself employable is to always be learning. So when the learning curve flattens out, Gen Y jumps."[16] When asked what would attract them, Millennials cited learning and development among the top three most important factors.[17]

Perhaps most telling are the comments from Millennials themselves. "When careers were based more on hierarchy, and work was more about getting a paycheck than knowledge, it didn't really matter what you did," says Gen Y blogger Rebecca Thorman. "But today's worker no longer desires swanky salaries or titles (although those don't hurt, certainly), but instead searches for work experiences that can contribute to their lives."[18]

The mind-set of people like Thorman is becoming more prevalent as younger generations constitute a larger percentage of the workforce. Younger workers don't believe, however, that they are entitled to growth without giving anything in return, as some observers mistakenly assume. To the contrary, they work hard in exchange for the right opportunities. And they are not alone: Generation X is particularly interested in continued professional development and in developing transferable skills.[19] "My father was a loyal corporate soldier who worked at the same company for 32 years," says Gen Xer Ryan Bristol, who left corporate America to become an entrepreneur. "But my generation is more interested in opportunities for fast growth than in security."[20] Overall, 97 percent of men and 90 percent of women are looking for "a range of new experiences" and say the main reason they would leave their current employer is a lack of these experiences.[21]

To respond to the careerquake, some companies are actively evolving into career-enhancing organizations. One early indicator: investments in career development and related training are growing faster than all other areas, including base pay.[22] Firms like QUAL-COMM, a $7.7 billion provider of wireless technology and services, are out in front. "We are very focused on employee development, because we realize the number one reason that people come to our organization is to develop themselves professionally," says Tamar Elkeles, vice president of learning and development. "Our focus on development is a key way that we retain talent. Today it isn't just about the money."[23]

The resurgence of job rotation programs also illustrates a move toward career enhancement, albeit in piecemeal programs rather than a fully integrated approach. Employers have expanded job rotation programs, with participation more than doubling over the past three years.[24] Such efforts are particularly popular with Gen Y.[25] Given estimates that 70 percent of learning comes from work experiences rather than education or other development programs, it is easy to understand the premium that employees place on the options offered by job rotations.[26] Employers value rotation programs, too, because they create the cross-departmental knowledge and relationships that spur collaboration. When the organization's right hand is well acquainted with its left hand, coordinated action leads to increased productivity.

Well-crafted job rotation programs are in operation at companies like General Electric and AT&T. At GE, new hires typically rotate into three or four assignments with a duration of six to eight months each. The goal is to accelerate the development of technical, business, and professional skills.[27] Recent graduates are hired directly into one of seven rotational programs in communication, engineering, finance, information management, operations management, technical sales, and human resources. Participants gain "accelerated experiences that would take years to gather in a standard corporate career."[28] And AT&T has developed a program that emulates an in-house temporary service. The program helps employees find short-term assignments to learn new skills and stay

Benefits of Career Enhancement

- Provides an appealing value proposition to attract and retain top talent

- Engages people through challenging assignments

- Builds capabilities the organization needs to compete

- Builds individuals' skills to maintain relevance in the changing marketplace

- Leverages work experiences for learning

- Rewards people in a currency they value: growth

---

challenged, and in return the "temps" offer fresh perspectives to the departments they support.[29] When done well, these career-enhancing programs prove that not all holdovers of the corporate ladder need be discarded—only viewed through a lattice lens.

Lockheed Martin showcases an even more integrated approach to career enhancement. It recognized that a lack of upward advancement options was hampering the development of its Gen X employees.[30] The $42 billion global security firm needed a new model for growth. The company instituted a multidimensional program in 2001 for its high-potential talent that includes rotations, tuition reimbursement, and mentoring pairs.

As a result, Lockheed has seen its turnover rate fall to only 2.5 percent.[31] Such low turnover is a competitive advantage in an industry in which 27 percent of aerospace and defense employees were eligible for retirement in 2008.[32] It's also an advantage for a defense contractor that increasingly competes with high-technology companies for workers who have science, technology, and engineering degrees.[33] "Recruiters try to woo you by offering more money, but it's really about a combination of things this company does, especially the emphasis on learning," says Ngina McLean, an engineering manager. "It's the only place I've worked where I can see spending my whole career."[34]

Career-enhancer organizations understand the value that talent places on the development of market-relevant skills, and the loyalty and high performance such transferable learning spurs.

Fitting Work into Life and Life into Work

Careers ebb and flow these days. That's because, as we describe in chapter 2, most families do not follow the traditional one-spouse-at-home-and-the-other-in-the-workforce model on which the corporate ladder was largely predicated. The number of working women with family responsibilities has mushroomed: the National Study of the Changing Workforce found that in 2007, 71 percent of mothers with children under age eighteen worked, up from 47 percent in 1975.[35] In fact, only about one in four Millennials had a stay-at-home mom, so it's not surprising that they place equal importance on career and family.[36] Nearly 60 percent of married couples in the United States are now dual income, and in almost 40 percent of families, women are the primary breadwinners.[37] These realities have major implications for the ways women *and* men think about career success.

Consider the case of "Robert." His career had a fairly typical start: he worked long hours, traveled every week, and earned steady promotions. But as his young family grew, Robert wanted to be home more nights for family dinners and bedtime tuck-ins, so he made a lateral move to a nonprofit professional association, where he could keep developing his skills with a more acceptable career–life fit. After his kids grew older, he moved back into a more demanding role and ultimately achieved a significant leadership position. As Robert puts it, "I would have liked options to remain with my employer and dial my career back for a time, but at the time there were few choices and none were socially acceptable for men to exercise."

Robert's story illustrates how people increasingly design job moves around life considerations rather than follow a strictly linear progression. A 2006 study by the Association of Executive Search Consultants confirmed that nearly nine out of ten people surveyed similarly considered work–life considerations an important factor in their career decisions.[38]

Men frequently follow Robert's path, leaving one company for another to dial their career up or down rather than risk the stigma associated with expressing a desire to better integrate career and life. One study found that 59 percent of men are interested in taking a break, but 75 percent believe a woman's request is more likely to be granted than a man's.[39] "When it comes to taking advantage of work-life policies, men encounter even more stigma [than women]," the study concludes. Men who ask for family leave are often made to feel that their commitment is in question, that their partners should dial down instead, and even that they're angling for more time off to relax and play golf. "If you're a man and you take flextime, the perception is that there's something really wrong with you," says Philip Reckers, an accounting professor at the W. P. Carey School of Business at Arizona State University and coauthor of a study of alternative work arrangements at four accounting firms.[40]

Women have long been making such trade-offs, regardless of the stigma the choices carry. Overall, the majority of U.S. women—60 percent—are considered to have nonlinear careers.[41] A task force that studies the "hidden brain drain" interviewed more than two thousand highly qualified women and found that 37 percent stopped working voluntarily; of these, 93 percent wanted to return to work after a short time out of the workforce averaging 2.2 years.[42] Additionally, another one-third of women will use some type of flexibility in how much, when, and where they work.[43]

Although women have been transitioning into and out of jobs more frequently than men, in another study the majority of men (58 percent) as well as women (68 percent) desire breaks rather than continuous, full-time work. "People who consider taking career breaks and who want more flexibility aren't an aberration, but instead reflect a broader overall shift in the traditional model of workday arrangements and a linear career path," the study concludes.[44]

Across the generations, for a variety of reasons, nonlinear careers are becoming the new normal. Boomers are at a life phase in which a different job experience is particularly appealing. More than 8 million, or 10 percent, of people between the ages of forty-four and seventy are involved in second, or "encore," careers, and half of the people in this age group who are not engaged in encore careers want to pursue them.[45] And 65 percent of working Baby Boomers say they are looking to better balance work and personal life.[46] Among younger workers, two-thirds of Generations X and Y say that they want to dial their jobs up or down in concert with their life needs.[47]

Clearly, across genders and generations, career–life fit has become a central requirement. As noted in chapter 1, career–life fit allows employees to find a sustainable, adaptive, and scalable way to fit life into work and work into life over time. And companies that integrate this kind of thinking throughout the organization find that it generates rather than detracts from high performance.

Indeed, almost half of employees in a 2009 Workplace Options survey said they would think about switching jobs for one that was more attractive from a work–life perspective.[48] Such results were particularly surprising during an economic downturn in which many people felt fortunate to have jobs at all.

American Family Insurance is one employer that is leading the way. For most of its eighty-two-year history, the $7 billion *Fortune* 500 company had a traditional approach to talent development, with management and employees focused primarily on vertical progression. But over the past seven years, the firm has been moving in a different direction. As talent management consultant Karla Walker explains, the company realized that not everyone viewed success as a vertical climb. "Through enlightenment and education, we are seeing a recognition that everybody does not aspire to move up and that we also need to support, encourage, and develop those individuals who are passionate about what they do and are very good at it."[49]

As part of the company's talent strategy, both high-potential employees and employees seeking growth experiences are moved laterally around the company to stretch them in areas in which they don't have experience. The company also enables its people to make choices that fit their personal needs. Continues Walker, "We have individuals at all levels who have said, 'I love what I do, but I need to pull back' because of their personal situation, and we facilitate that happening. We have multiple options to grow, such as job rotations, coaching, and mentoring, and those options are more acceptable in the organization than ever before." Moves up continue to be possible, but the company also understands that people may want to take a step sideways or down to gain what they need.

American Family exemplifies how to offer a variety of growth and career–life options that engage individuals having different perspectives of success. At the same time, this practice fosters a new mind-set that better aligns the needs and expectations of both the workforce and the workplace.

ADVANCING LATTICE WAYS TO BUILD CAREERS

Because necessity is the mother of invention, individuals often feel they must unilaterally come up with solutions to meet their own career and life needs. Some organizations are now beginning to craft workarounds to address their employees' concerns. But they are, by and large, creating one-off solutions—such as flexible work arrangements, mobility programs, or learning activities—that lack integration with each other or with existing business processes like performance management and career planning. The result is a patchwork of programs that lags behind the evolution of the talent market. To help them catch up, we offer two practical tools that expand choices to the mutual benefit of employees and employers.

Mapping Out Multiple Pathways

Lattice career moves are likely becoming more commonplace in your organization. In an ad hoc fashion, forward-thinking managers might work out a nontraditional career move to retain a high performer or meet an urgent business issue, with both parties working out a tactical remedy to solve an immediate crisis. By using the *lattice career pathways* tool, however, companies and their employees can intentionally think through and collaboratively map out talent development, formalizing it, scaling it, and making it more equitable. Lattice pathways help employees and managers visualize and plan customized growth trajectories while increasing transparency about choices and trade-offs. At the same time, they offer firms more options for deploying talent and keeping pace with volatile business conditions than does the ladder's rung-by-rung mode of progression.

This road map (see an example in figure 3-1) charts potential choices for moving laterally, growing in place, and moving up. Each box shows the level and type of position—such as management, expert, or a hybrid—so that various career models are captured and ultimately considered. The diagram includes traditional vertical moves that represent the development of increasingly higher levels of mastery in leadership or in depth of expertise, as well as various lateral moves that may rely on transferable skills and experience between two roles. Many firms also designate "career" positions in which an individual might choose to remain

FIGURE 3-1

Lattice pathways example

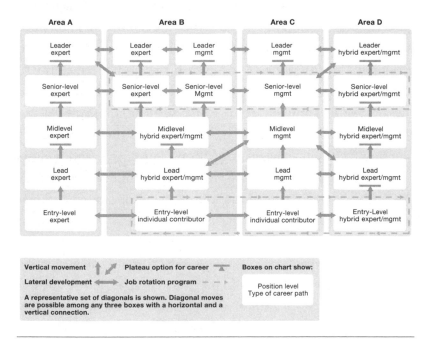

Vertical movement ↑↗ Plateau option for career ⊥ Boxes on chart show:

Lateral development ⟷ Job rotation program --→

A representative set of diagonals is shown. Diagonal moves are possible among any three boxes with a horizontal and a vertical connection.

Position level
Type of career path

for an extended period, perhaps because of life needs or simply based on personal and organizational preferences.

What's the upside of mapping out career pathways? We think that when individuals and managers can picture the possibilities, their perception of option value rises, as explained in chapter 1. Lattice pathways visibly demonstrate leadership's commitment to talent development and support for a career–life fit that works for each individual as well as the organization. They also help managers and employees have rich counseling discussions, because everyone is talking about the same set of possibilities. And once written down, lattice pathways can be shared with potential recruits as a marketing tool to attract people to the company. Perhaps the tougher question is, Why not diagram career pathways?

Another purpose of lattice pathways is to lay out career routes to guide the development of expert knowledge workers. Peter

Drucker, who is largely credited with coining the term *knowledge worker,* posited that knowledge work was central to any firm's ability to compete in the twenty-first century.[50] Management guru Thomas Davenport estimates that the number of knowledge workers ranges from a quarter to half of workers in developed economies, and he argues that "even if they're not a majority of all workers . . . they add the most economic value, and they are the greatest determinant of the worth of their companies."[51] Yet traditional career ladders are not attuned to this reality, often focusing on the management of people, processes, and budgets rather than knowledge. As one group of academics notes, "Expertise is the key currency of the knowledge economy and expert *discretion* provides perhaps the critical source of knowledge in organizations."[52]

A major drawback of the ladder model is that it does not adequately develop specialists who may have deep expertise, institutional knowledge, or critical relationships, nor does it readily adapt when new types of skills emerge. Kevin Wilde, chief learning officer at General Mills, gives a simple example of how this plays out: "One of the trends General Mills and other companies are facing is that because new things are emerging all the time, destination jobs aren't as clear as they were. For example, as digital media has become a key way for us to connect with our consumers, we are developing a career model for digital media expertise that didn't exist ten years ago."[53] Given the growth in specialist positions, a company's failure to address these unique routes to success is increasingly a deficiency.

Another downside is the ladder model's rigid expectation about how individuals should progress. For example, in the consumer goods industry, a vertical progression might include such positions as marketing analyst, assistant brand manager, brand manager, assistant marketing director, marketing director, and, ultimately, general manager. Whether or not it is expressly stated, these steps typically contain an "up or out" component, meaning that an individual who moves too slowly is considered off track and may be moved out or sidelined—sometimes graciously, sometimes not.

Lattice career pathways provide flexibility, enabling knowledge workers to customize their journeys over time, and companies to deepen their on-demand pool of expertise. These pathways illuminate options along the corporate lattice. They differ from ladder career paths in several key respects.

- **Expert-role pathways often coexist with traditional management paths:** A variety of hybrid roles may exist as well, providing choices for individuals and organizations to meet shifting life and market needs.

- **Roles connect laterally as well as vertically:** Lateral moves and the transferable skills they enable are valued because they multiply options for talent development, address issues created by flatter structures, and seed the cross-silo knowledge and relationships that fuel collaboration.

- **"Up or out" is out:** Decoupling progression from tenure recognizes the importance of building deep expertise over time, acknowledges that individuals learn at different speeds, and allows for options to grow at faster or slower rates at different stages in life.

Examples of fluid career lattices are emerging across the business landscape. In information technology, career pathways are a best practice that suits the field's knowledge-dependent work. On a recent blog posting, an anonymous worker wrote, "All the companies that I have worked for over the years have no concept of a technical career path . . . in which a designer/coder/architect such as myself can continue to advance his career, yet stay doing what they love. Instead, they expect you to become a manager, pushing paper (or e-mails these days), managing budgets, going to meetings, and delegating tasks. Everything I don't want to do. What career ladder have you seen that did allow a developer to remain a

Features of Lattice Career Pathways

- Create multidirectional development options, expanding choices for individualized career moves

- Provide transparency about the range of possible roles, along with the benefits and trade-offs

- Focus the culture less on upward moves and more on development and contribution

- Build cross-silo relationships and knowledge, thereby improving collaboration, coordination, and execution

developer without dead-ending their advancement?" The person's posting elicited a host of replies, offering only isolated anecdotes of success.[54]

Nevertheless, the field is gradually improving. Standard Life, for example, has expert development routes. Keith Young, the head of IT, believes these options avoid the situation where "if a good technician moves into a senior management role, we can lose a good developer and gain a poor manager."[55] Many IT roles today have transferable skills that enable lateral moves to business roles and back to IT again.

The Council for Adult and Experiential Learning (CAEL) is another organization that has developed a lattice pathways model to address the shortage of nurses in the United States. The aging of the Baby Boomers is expected to produce a shortfall of 260,000 registered nurses in the United States by 2025, double the size of any shortage since the 1960s.[56] The government-funded CAEL program was designed to recruit a broad range of workers to become certified nurse assistants (CNAs), a gateway position to a variety of health care jobs. The CAEL project says it adopted the metaphor of a lattice because "careers do not always follow straight lines" as workers make lateral moves as well as vertical steps in and out of occupations.[57]

"The lattice notion came about because we recognized that once people had preliminary training, they might discover they wanted a role with less patient care, such as a laboratory or surgical technician position," says Phyllis Snyder, vice president of CAEL. "We wanted to provide a road map for horizontal movement in the health care environment. The important thing was that by coming into a CNA position, they were opening up to a lattice of jobs, not simply a linear path."[58] The model was rolled out to more than fifteen states, and additional sites used do-it-yourself published materials to implement similar programs. Although the tracking of results varied according to the sponsoring employer, benefits included reduced patient waiting times and improved patient satisfaction.[59]

Global law firm Orrick, Herrington, Sutcliffe LLP also launched a new talent model in 2009 that offers a wide array of career options. This move was, in part, a strategic response to two key marketplace issues: dissatisfaction by clients with the price–value ratios of legal service providers, and significant changes in the expectations of law school graduates who want varying career choices.

"The lockstep system [that] law firms use to manage careers and compensate associates just doesn't make sense, because people wind up progressing according to the calendar and not according to their professional development," explains Ralph Baxter, CEO of Orrick.[60] "The lockstep model inhibited our ability to provide more attractive pricing to our clients, and it didn't create the right career incentives for lawyers. Associates seemed frustrated by their careers instead of being excited in the way that I remembered being when I was a young associate." Explains Katharine Crost, a partner in Orrick's financial markets practice, "The traditional linear career model was not maximizing the return on talent development investments for the firm."[61]

Orrick's model now provides a variety of career options rather than a single, linear path to partner.[62] Advancement is now performance based rather than tenure based, with specific core competency criteria to guide decisions. As a result, the pace of each career is individualized. A custom career track allows individuals to tailor their development based on their career interests and goals as well as life needs.

"The model recognizes that moving forward in one's development is not limited to moving upward on the traditional career ladder," says Laura Saklad, chief lawyer development officer. "There are many ways of progressing one's career and contributing meaningful value to the organization."[63] Compensation has also changed to enable the new approach. Rather than being based on billable hours or firm profitability, bonuses are based on quality, efficiency, and contribution. "Changing the bonus structure is an important step, because we're then aligning with what the clients want us to care about and aligning with the way we want our model to be," concludes Baxter.[64]

By providing a map of opportunities, lattice career pathways help individuals take greater ownership of their careers. With an increased number of options, employees can customize work to suit their individual circumstances while developing the capabilities the firm needs.

Normalizing Customized Careers

Some companies have transformed their approach to careers by leveraging the principles of customization. The mass career customization (MCC) tool provides a framework, a process, and a road map to personalize careers, making career development collaborative and dynamic. Unlike flexible work arrangements, which represent an "opt in" approach that often leads to feelings of exception or accommodation, everyone in a company participates in the MCC process all the time. It institutionalizes and

FIGURE 3-2

The MCC profile has four interrelated dimensions

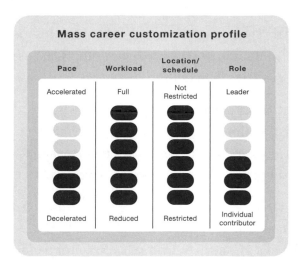

The MCC framework takes into account growth and development along with career–life fit at the individual and organizational levels. It provides a systematic approach to identify options, make choices, and agree on trade-offs. MCC articulates a definite, not infinite, set of options along four interrelated dimensions of a career: Pace, Workload, Location/Schedule, and Role. Each is a continuum of defined levels, as shown in figure 3-2.

These dimensions represent generic elements of a career. Companies can tailor them to best fit their environment. (These details are explored in the book *Mass Career Customization*.[65]). For discussion purposes, we define the dimensions as follows.

- **Pace:** How quickly individuals develop and grow both in an absolute sense and relative to their peers. People sometimes dial up their pace by taking stretch assignments to accelerate growth, or they dial down to address life needs and interests—in both cases to align with their own models of success.

- **Workload:** The quantity of work performed. Most people select a full-time workload, whereas others dial down to something less than full-time.

- **Location/Schedule:** Options for where and when work is performed. Options may include working remotely some or all of the time and varying schedules to, for example, start and end early or have a compressed workweek.

- **Role:** The category of an employee's position, job description, and responsibilities. In some firms, the Role continuum ranges from an individual contributor performing specific tasks to a management position, or it could represent a continuum of activity between external client-facing and internal staff-oriented positions. How companies design lattice career pathways also shapes Role definitions.

The MCC profile provides a snapshot of each employee's career at a given point, and it can be modified over time. Just as you would adjust the sound on a stereo equalizer by moving the sliders up or down, the MCC framework and process allow employees, in collaboration with their managers, to dial their careers up or down at varying life stages. The four dimensions are interrelated, and a change in one usually affects one or more of the others. In this way, the MCC approach improves the transparency of trade-offs among options, giving employees the information they need to make sound decisions and avoiding misunderstandings that can create mistrust down the road.

An MCC profile captures an individual's career–life options at a moment in time. At different career and life stages, individuals often make different choices. By positioning profiles for each career stage side by side, employees can see how levels of career engage-ment evolve over time in tandem with life needs. We have dubbed the resulting line-up a *career sine wave*. Figure 3-3 depicts a compos-ite of career journeys that we've seen plotted as a career sine wave.

Even though the path depicted here is individually customized, note that the MCC tool does not open the door to an infinite number of choices. It enables companies to define choices that can be mixcd and matched to create work options that are com-patible with the business and that employees will value.

MCC is an integrative framework rather than a stand-alone program. It ties together existing talent practices, such as the lat-tice pathways described earlier, work–life benefits and initiatives, individual learning plans, high-potential development efforts, and performance management, for example. The MCC profile provides a context for agreeing on goals and expectations related to a person's level of contribution.

The experience of Thrivent Financial for Lutherans shows how one company used the MCC tool to redesign its approach to careers. With five thousand employees, the *Fortune* 500 financial services firm helps 2.6 million members achieve their financial goals.[66] In 2006, Thrivent Financial launched an ambitious agenda: to double its most engaged membership. This goal would shift its focus from products to long-term, service-based relationships.

To deliver on its business strategy, Thrivent Financial realized it needed to develop a corresponding talent strategy that focused on developing deep, long-term relationships with its people. A cor-nerstone of the strategy was to build "a 'career culture' in which employees would feel empowered to achieve their aspirations," explains Barbara Foote, vice president, enterprise effectiveness and talent office.[67] People needed to see how they could grow over time at Thrivent Financial. Its organizational structure had become rela-tively flat, and that limited vertical progression opportunities, so it needed to improve the perceived value of lateral moves.

FIGURE 3-3

Career engagement changes over time

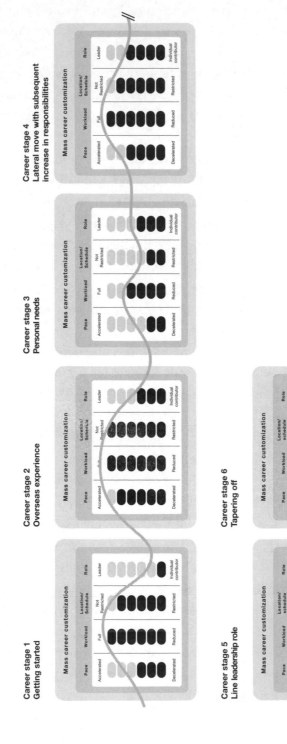

Features of the Mass Career Customization Tool

- Recognizes that careers ebb and flow over time

- Provides a scalable, equitable system of flexibility

- Emphasizes that options need to work for the business and the employee

- Moves from one-off exceptions and accommodations to "all in"

- Provides transparency about trade-offs while enabling a sustainable career–life fit

- Integrates with existing talent processes

Thrivent Financial recognized that some midcareer employees were feeling that their careers had stalled when only lateral moves were available. The integration of career and life was also important, both because of its consistency with the company's deeply held values and because of its alignment with the demographic transformation of workers.

Called the Thrivent Career GPS, the effort has three components:

- The *goals and values* that people aspire to in their professional and personal lives

- The *profile* of life and work

- The *sweet spot,* or the intersection of a person's strengths and passions and the needs of the business

To develop its profiles of life and work, the "P" in GPS, Thrivent Financial used the MCC tool and tailored it to its business. It found that the four core dimensions of the tool resonated with its implementation team, and the company then developed definitions for each dimension that aligned with its needs and culture, as shown in figure 3-4.

To implement the GPS framework, Thrivent Financial staggered its rollout, beginning in marketing in early 2008 and then expanding.[68] What it has learned from each phase has been used to improve the next implementation. Marketing was a natural place to start, because its leadership was particularly committed to the vision, and, even though its employees were highly engaged, they expressed a need for more career development. Next, the HR

FIGURE 3-4

Thrivent's customized MCC profile

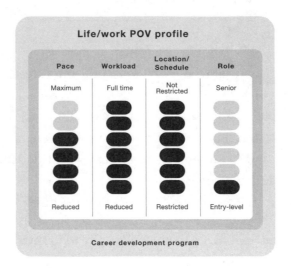

Pace: Preferences related to the rate of career development experiences

Workload: Preferences related to the quantity of work expected

Location/Schedule: Preferences for when and where work is performed

Role: Preferences related to career track, such as technical path or general management path

Source: Thrivent Financial.

department rolled out GPS, in part to provide the HR team with firsthand experience in working with the new model as well as to improve how careers are built for Thrivent Financial's HR professionals.[69]

The team used a high-touch process to help drive cultural change. It held workshops for managers and employees to educate them on the framework and its business rationale. To show that the corporate lattice was already happening informally, leaders also commissioned case studies of people within Thrivent Financial who had built lattice-like careers. About 10 percent of those in the rollouts chose to dial up or down, in roughly equal numbers, illustrating that most employees choose the common profile at any given point in time.[70]

Surveys conducted before and after the marketing rollout have been promising. Among other results, they showed a 9 percent increase in satisfaction with Thrivent Financial's opportunities for development.[71] The company reports that GPS has enabled people to have transparent conversations about their needs, and managers say that their conversations with employees have been much richer and deeper than they were in the past. Managers and their staffs are also more open to lateral moves than they were before. "Prior to GPS, lateral moves had some stigma associated with them," explains Foote. "Now we are seeing the culture change. Managers and employees are talking about lateral options, and employees who make lateral moves to grow their career are being talked about as role models."[72] In fact, Thrivent Financial began to measure lateral moves and saw a steady upward trend.

Following the success of the original pilots, GPS implementation was extended to Thrivent Financial's corporate real estate and banking groups as of mid-2009. And the company continues to explore how it can expand its lattice model and take advantage of what it is learning through the implementation of career customization. For example, it is interested in understanding how the design of work shapes the relationship between the high performance and career–life fit of its financial field representatives, a customer-facing role that is vital to the company's growth strategy.

Thrivent Financial's experience highlights important learnings for an effective implementation. One pitfall that befalls some companies is that efforts turn into bureaucratic "check the box" exercises. Thrivent Financial, however, puts interaction and dialogue front and center. The company understands employee–manager conversations are the real enabler of customization.

Companies should also change their thinking and move away from labeling choices to vary career growth from traditional, ladder norms as "exceptions." Given the normal inertia of change efforts, it is easy to stigmatize personal choices. The goal is to make integrating career and life part of business as usual. Investment in the education of leaders and managers is essential to move their thinking forward.

The Thrivent Financial experience confirms that the MCC framework is a practical, sustainable, and scalable tool for building a lattice organization. It requires investment and leadership to succeed in helping change mind-sets and create new patterns for building careers. In return, MCC attracts and engages talent and builds a company's reputation as an employer of choice.

———————

By making good use of the lattice career pathways and mass career customization tools, companies can engage people across a broad spectrum of individual ideas about success. Lattice organizations are turning next to the myriad ways people are working within the organization. As careers are being remade, the workplace, where those careers take flight, is also being redesigned. Lattice ways to work are enabling expanded career options. And as chapter 4 shows, work today is nothing like it was in the past.

4 ▶ LATTICE WAYS TO WORK

What worked yesterday is the gilded cage of tomorrow.

—*Peter Block*

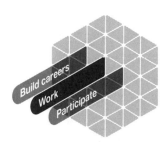

N THE LATTICE WORLD, the phrase "9 to 5" more aptly describes a campy 1980s film than the workplace today. The "when, where, and how" of work are different now, owing in large part to profound shifts in technological and economic forces.

Work is increasingly virtual, dispersed, and 24/7. The transition to a knowledge economy has made a great deal of work less repetitive and more dependent on a highly educated workforce. Jobs are less structured, and the pace is faster. Companies are often neutral to location and time zone and deploy project teams and task forces that cut across departmental silos and organizational levels. Employees have more choices about how to work and are expected to exhibit greater initiative in achieving results.

Lattice organizations are not simply reacting to these forces but rather are redesigning the foundations of work itself. In the process, they are customizing the workplace to deliver both high performance for their shareholders and sustainable career–life fit for their talent. "More flexible ways to work are a path to better performance, to better productivity, to better returns for the corporation," says Xerox chairman Anne Mulcahy. "This is a way of improving business results rather than just a way to accommodate employees' personal lives."[1]

THE NEW TERRAIN OF WORK

People work in many more varied ways than in the past. Telecommuting, modular job and process designs, global teams working around the clock on projects, matrix-driven organizational models and management styles, expanded options for customizing work—although uncommon even twenty years ago, these practices are fast becoming the norm. The result is that ladder thinking about work is giving way to lattice thinking (see table 4-1).

Flexible ways of working expand options for building careers. Together, work and careers strengthen a company's talent brand: in a 2008 survey, 70 percent of professionals said that flexibility is the deciding nonmonetary factor in picking a job.[2] And, as you will see in chapter 5, lattice ways of working provide the infrastructure on which firms construct lattice ways of participating.

In this chapter we explore the transformation of work and offer implementation steps companies can take to effectively navigate the workplace terrain.

When and Where Work Gets Done

Across industries, a wide range of work options spans time and location. For example:

- ASDA, a U.K. supermarket chain with 313 stores and 150,000 employees, set up a system that allows workers

TABLE 4-1

A comparison of ladder and lattice thinking about work

Ladder work norms	Lattice work norms
Work is a place you go	Work is what you do
9-to-5 hours	24/7 hours
Work design is often repetitive and routine	Work design is often nonroutine and responsive to market issues and opportunities
Work is often structured around individual contributions and results	Work is often structured around team-based contributions and results
Job responsibilities are relatively static	Job responsibilities are fluid
Job descriptions provide boundaries to work within	Job descriptions are based on competencies required to meet business objectives
Teams often are co-located, permanent, and work within an organizational area	Teams are often far-flung, transitory, and work across organizational silos
Management dictates the when, where, and how of work	Employees have choices, within guidelines, about the when, where, and how of work

to swap shifts and even to switch stores if workers were moving from one location to another. In addition to the flexibility employees gain when they can customize when and where they work, the business found that workers "up-skilled" as they learned additional roles, and managers were "better able to match staff to peak hours and seasonal variations."[3]

- 1-800 CONTACTS, a direct-to-consumer retailer of contact lenses, invested in systems that allow agents to manage orders without having to work in a corporate office, so nearly 50 percent of their call-center staff work from home. The company also created a proprietary software program to manage hundreds of flexible schedules for its agents.

As a result, turnover rates are two-thirds lower than the industry national average, and in 2007 J.D. Power & Associates gave 1-800 CONTACTS its "highest service rating ever for a call center."[4]

- With twenty-nine thousand employees, Capital One is one of the largest banks in the United States. It launched a program that equips associates with technology to virtually connect them from home and provide choices about when and where they work. On occasions when telecommuters do come into the office, they are assigned an available workspace. Results have impressed employees and management alike: Capital One cut occupancy costs, and high numbers of employees reported greater satisfaction and increased productivity from the arrangement.[5]

These are only a few examples of forward-looking organizations that let employees customize when and where work gets done. The facts also show that such efforts are rapidly gaining ground: of more than two thousand U.S. employers surveyed in 2008, 42 percent said they allow remote work, a significant rise from the 30 percent that did so in 2007.[6] And 83 percent of companies ranked on the *Fortune* 100 Best Companies to Work For list incorporate virtual work options.[7]

People are still working at the office, to be sure, but they are also working from home, from the coffee shop, on the train, and lots of places in between. And when employees come to the office, they are likely to experience an environment that is much more flexibly configured than traditional offices. Why? Because as many as 70 percent of employees' jobs are now done collaboratively.[8] Capital One, for example, is forgoing traditional offices and cubicles for contemporary combinations of conference areas, shared desks, and even sofas.[9]

Indeed, about three-quarters of *Fortune* 500 companies already offer unassigned workstations.[10] In the office environment, as many as 40 percent of physical workspaces, on average, are vacant on any given business day, so the potential for savings in real estate and physical infrastructure costs is huge.[11] By moving to open office designs, companies such as Motorola and Cisco are significantly reducing real estate costs, in some cases saving as much as 40 percent.[12] And Sprint Nextel's "Work Anywhere" model has helped the company release more than 3 million square feet of office space since 2005, with projected annual savings of $80 million beginning in 2009.[13] During 2008, five thousand employees' workspaces became "Sprint mobile zones," which integrate real estate design, technology tools, and human resource policies and are tailored to each work group. As a result, employee productivity is up 30 percent—equivalent to more than $4 million of annual revenue.[14]

People frequently work at all hours, too, in part to accommodate their colleagues around the world. Rather than go to the gym in the early morning, team members in New York schedule calls with colleagues in Frankfurt but then take an hour later in the day to get their workout in. While workers may not mind converting some of their evening, weekend, or wee morning hours to work time, in return they expect flexibility in customizing their schedules to allow breaks during traditional work hours.

Benefits of Customizing the "When and Where" of Work

- Lowers real estate and related overhead costs

- Raises employee productivity and lowers absenteeism

- Improves the attraction and retention of talent

- Reduces both the individual's and the organization's carbon footprint

- Lowers the risk of business interruption

Organizations that adopt lattice thinking enable workers to customize when and where work is done and, in turn, maximize benefits to both the individual and the business. The most obvious benefit to employees is a higher degree of day-to-day flexibility, or what TV anchors and authors Claire Shipman and Katty Kay call "work–life" *control*.[15] This practice allows people to successfully manage the daily demands of work and life, whether it is working from home when a child is sick or conferencing in from the repair shop while the car is being fixed.

Additional benefits to the individual and to society include reduced commuting costs and lowered environmental impact. The National Science Foundation estimates that each of its teleworkers saves about $1,200 a year in gas and other expenses.[16] Researcher Chris Park, a leading industry consultant in the field of corporate sustainability, has estimated that commuting represents up to 20 percent of a person's carbon footprint. Flexible work options can have a material impact on individual "greening" efforts.[17]

Just as individuals gain from additional choices, organizations also benefit. A decrease in energy use from telework results in lower carbon emissions, which can generate salable offsets for companies under carbon-trading schemes.[18] The Telework Exchange estimated that telework in the federal government reduced air pollutants by more than 24 million pounds.[19]

In addition, employers gain options for business continuity during emergencies. Companies in lower Manhattan faced the sudden loss of not only lives but also workplaces after the terrorist attacks of September 11, 2001. One investment bank realized that it was able to resume business rapidly in part because employees were already working from home. A year later, the bank was encouraging office-based employees to telecommute at least one day a month "to make sure they have the know-how to keep working if headquarters is closed."[20] A related component of business continuity planning is *social distancing* which reduces physical contact during disease outbreaks similar to the H1N1 flu pandemic of 2009. Remote work infrastructure helps with this, too.

Flexibility retains employees and helps them be more productive. Research concludes that when employees can adequately manage their work and personal lives, they take less time off and are more loyal. BT, the British telecommunications giant, has found that its teleworkers take 63 percent less sick time, and the return rate of women from maternity leave is 99 percent, versus the average return rate in the United Kingdom of 47 percent.[21] The more employees are focused on their jobs rather than worried about their personal lives, the more efficiently they get things done. AT&T has saved $150 million annually through teleworking, and $100 million of this savings is attributed to increased employee productivity.[22]

The United States Patent and Trademark Office (USPTO) experienced precisely these benefits when it moved in 2006 to a comprehensive telework approach that offers a variety of programs tailored to the needs of seven different business groups. USPTO provides equal access to information systems whether a patent examiner is working in an office or remotely; focuses on performance and results; and offers strong leadership from the top in support of telework. In the four years before the program was implemented, "one patent examiner left for every two the agency hired."[23] Largely as a result of the teleworking effort, the agency has improved the retention of its talent. Three-fourths of patent examiners now say that the telecommuting program is an important or very important reason to remain at USPTO.

One year after USPTO rolled out its program, an impressive four out of ten employees were participating in some form of remote work, making it one of the largest efforts in the federal government. The agency has saved millions of dollars in real estate costs, lowered carbon emissions, and increased productivity 10 percent— all with no negative impact on the quality of work. Its move toward lattice ways of working also enhanced lattice ways to build careers. *BusinessWeek* recognized USPTO as one of the Best Places to Launch a Career, *Washington Family Magazine* and named it one of the best employers in the Washington area for working families.[24]

Such results are not limited to organizations with highly skilled workers. A large study of hourly workers found a significant increase in engagement and a decrease in turnover among those who had the flexibility they needed to manage their schedules.[25]

How Work Gets Done

Not only are expectations about the "when and where" of work changing, but also the nature of work is evolving. Technology has fueled this decades-long evolution: in addition to providing platforms that connect employees across time and place, technological advances are digitizing many work processes. The result is an increased demand for a broad, dynamic range of organization and employee capabilities. Information analysis, innovation, and adaptability, for example, are competencies that are growing in importance as companies adapt to markets that are changing at accelerating rates.

Routine work that's highly structured and repetitive is being replaced by nonroutine tasks that require greater autonomy and critical thinking skills (see figure 4-1). Job descriptions are also becoming more malleable; many companies today define jobs according to the competencies a worker needs rather than defining the job as a static list of tasks.

For many people, titles and job descriptions no longer precisely define their work. "It's almost like you have to embrace a lot of ambiguity and be adaptable and not get into the rigidness or expectation-setting that I think there used to be 10 years ago, when you could plot out where you were going to go," says Xerox's Mulcahy. "It's a lot more fluid right now. It has to be. The people who really do the best are those who actually sense, and enjoy

FIGURE 4-1

Trends in nonroutine and routine tasks

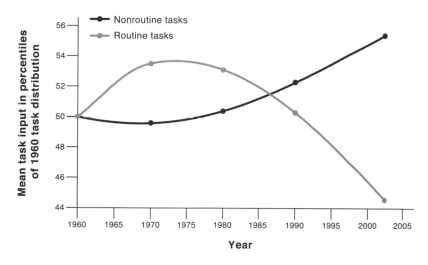

Source: Gene Grossman and Esteban Rossi-Hansberg, "The Rise of Offshoring: It's Not Wine for Cloth Anymore," *Proceedings* (Kansas City: Federal Reserve Bank of Kansas City, 2006).

almost, that lack of definition around their roles and what they can contribute."[26]

Employees today are more often called upon to exercise levels of judgment that exceed their rank in the official hierarchy. They are expected to take greater initiative in achieving the goals their managers establish. Globalization is one driver of this expanded autonomy, and it is even changing the premise of how managers manage. At the Thomson Reuters U.K.-based sales and trading division, for example, 40 percent of staff live outside the country in which their manager works.[27] "Those managers who subscribed to managing by walking around had to change the most," says Matthew Burkley, chief financial officer of the division. When managers are not located with their teams and often work in different time zones, they depend on employees to act.

General Mills' Mike Davis has a similar take: "We're really having to learn how to change our work processes so that you can have people halfway around the globe working on the same thing. Our global teams are telling us the work process has to change, because if team members have to wait to check in on every step, they lose a whole day waiting for replies on check-ins across time zones."[28]

Pitney Bowes has adopted these concepts as the underpinnings of its transformation from a product company selling postage meters to a solutions company helping customers manage their "mailstream." For most of its history (more than one hundred years), the company manufactured and serviced postage machines. Its workforce was highly segregated among employees in factories, customer service, and management. Most factory workers performed a single task in the line, usually from memory. Their work was repetitive and routine. By the mid-1990s, newly appointed (and since retired) CEO Mike Critelli had intensified the company's focus on mailstream management, with greater investments in technology to produce digital mail machines customized to customer specifications. This shift changed the "how" of the company's work, because building and servicing the new machines involved a high level of interaction with customers and was technically more complicated than in the past.[29]

The transformation required a fundamental change in the company's operations, starting at the factory floor and moving all the way to the top. Factory workers were rearranged into self-directed teams that read blueprints and did troubleshooting in real time. Factory foremen learned how to be coaches who inspired teams to perform, no longer relying on a command-and-control approach. Engineers and the sales force, and eventually even the finance and marketing departments, switched from a task-based view to a results-driven, team-based one.

Pitney Bowes is not alone in sensing the need to operate differently. A number of companies have adopted flexible teams as their basic operating unit. Companies use cross-functional project teams that form and disband as needed instead of having tasks move serially from department to department. "As companies become more global enterprises, careers are increasingly being built on demonstrating skills at marshaling resources of more temporary teams than permanent structures," says General Mills' Davis.[30] Notes Pfizer's Tanya Clemons, "It stands to reason that being continually adaptive in response to the ever-changing marketplace requires three things: more autonomy on the part of the individual, greater global collaboration among virtual team members, and a vast proliferation of project-based work."[31]

Indeed, the average number of projects has increased fortyfold in the past two decades.[32] The United States had almost 8 million project workers in 2006, with 1.2 million net job openings in project-based industries likely each year until 2016.[33] To put it in monetary terms, the Project Management Institute estimates that approximately one-fifth of global GDP spending, or about $12 trillion, is now spent on fixed-capital projects such as power plants and factories.[34]

For most of the twentieth century, companies were organized in either functional silos or individual business units (or both). As an early sign of the emerging lattice, starting in the 1970s companies began to adopt a matrix organizational structure to increase information sharing and speed the assignment of resources to new areas. In contrast to a functional organization, where an employee has one manager and is a member of one department like sales or production, employees in a matrix structure often have one "solid line" and other "dotted line" bosses. For example, a salesperson might have one reporting line up to the head of sales and a second reporting line to the regional manager. People work in cross-functional teams by the very design of the matrix structure.

Matrix organizations bring with them their own set of challenges—including, at times, employees' receiving conflicting directions from multiple bosses, a lack of single-point accountability for success or failure, and political infighting over resources. But matrices provide compelling benefits too. They promote collaborative working styles and enable business decisions that consider multiple perspectives such as function, product, customer, and geography.

Lattice organizations foster these positive behaviors along horizontal structures, bringing the best resources and information to bear on intersecting issues and opportunities. For example, widely dispersed virtual teams—often with a variety of experts based in different global locations—are delivering strong results. Fifty-four global teams studied in thirty-one companies, including Intel, Textronic, and Royal Dutch/Shell, were found to be not only more productive but also more innovative than face-to-face teams. According to the study, "Far-flung global teams make decisions faster with more input from others and develop policies that are implemented worldwide with fewer problems than conventional teams meeting face-to-face often and regularly." Teams find productive ways to communicate, partner together, and tap in to the power of diversity.[35] As we detail in the next chapter, collaboration is an important enabler of dispersed ways of working.

In addition to capitalizing on the best qualities of matrix reporting structures and far-flung team configurations, lattice organizations are going even further along the path of job redesign. Just as an easily reconfigurable production system is a success factor for mass product customization, so too is the design of *modularized* jobs—unbundling activities that make up traditional jobs so that work can be allocated in a greater variety of ways among team members, increasing opportunities for efficiency, learning, and fit with life—a key element of the lattice organization.[36] Static, task-based job descriptions are being replaced with competency-based descriptions to provide more adaptability in how work is divvied up and accomplished from one day to the next. Job modularization is also enabled by team-based control and decision making about how projects get done and who is responsible for which piece.

The film business is an example of a highly adaptable and fluid work structure. The entire industry is project based, with teams composed of "diversely skilled members who work for a limited period to create custom and complex products or services."[37] One study showed that only 19 percent of people in the industry were employed exclusively by one firm.[38] The rest worked as subcontractors and had "boundaryless careers." Team members decide among themselves how to accomplish the tasks at hand, customizing the fit between work assignments and individual abilities and circumstances. The needs of the business and the needs of the individual are matched in real time.

The lattice organization rethinks who does what, with an eye toward making movement across and within teams as seamless as possible. Given the highly contextual nature of how and what work gets done, a company's task is to provide teams with the tools needed to manage the right match between the company's needs, the capabilities of team members, their career–life needs, and the career-enhancing developmental opportunities that projects afford. "Work units have to collectively make these decisions, and they have to make them based both on the needs of the work and the needs of the employees," explains Lotte Bailyn, a professor at the MIT Sloan School of Management. "It can't be done individually. It has to be done collectively by the people who work interdependently. It needs to involve people in decisions about how to get a product or service out productively and address the needs they have in conjunction with achieving this result."[39]

One example of the approach is physicians, who among the elite professions have the highest proportion of people working fewer than thirty-five hours a week beginning in their late thirties. Doctors' ability to work part-time later on seems to be a payoff for the grueling hours of residency early in their careers, and it appears to ease transitions between periods of working and not working. Economist Claudia Goldin and her colleagues at Harvard

University found that doctors move in and out of the labor force, interrupting their careers for a year or more at a time, with far less financial penalty than in other professions, such as financial services and law.[40]

Such career–life transitions are possible because of a restructuring of the way work is done in many medical specialties. Instead of going solo in individual practices, doctors are often employed in group practices, which function as teams that jointly configure their schedules to provide high levels of accessibility and quality care for patients at a sustainable pace and workload for doctors. In obstetrics, for instance, doctors in group practices take turns handling the demanding times they need to be on call for births and sometimes rotate the patients so that women get to know every doctor who might eventually deliver their babies. Medical practices like these have, surprisingly for the nature of the work, turned out to be models of group work and flexibility.

Redesigning jobs so that people can more readily move from one job to another greatly enables career–life fit, but it also delivers on the career-enhancing developmental opportunities people seek. A large-scale study of functional flexibility—conducted at thirty-six hundred Dutch companies employing more than eleven thousand people in a variety of industries—showed "a positive relationship between functional flexibility and skills development," in large part because people felt they had "greater autonomy in directing their skills, involvement in decision-making, and access to training."[41] In another example, three health care organizations in the United Kingdom changed their approach to staffing so that many of their people could step into several different roles, depending on the need for workers at any point in time. These organizations found that the arrangement created increased opportunities for staff development—a competitive advantage in a tight labor market.[42] As market uncertainties rise, companies look for options to deploy their people. By designing jobs with an eye toward development of transferable skills, companies gain adaptability.

Benefits of Redesigning How Work Is Done

- Improves adaptability and speed

- Increases productivity

- Enhances responsiveness to customers

- Develops transferable skills

- Expands choices for career–life fit

Rethinking work creates a nimble organization that can operate with efficiency and effectiveness. In the case of Pitney Bowes, the work redesign led the entire organization to be more customer-focused and ultimately more profitable than before. According to Amy Titus, a former BearingPoint consultant who was involved in the Pitney Bowes transformation, the shift resulted in "everyone in the chain adding more value, in part because they understood customer needs, and in part because they were much more engaged in their work."[43]

ADVANCING LATTICE WAYS OF WORKING

Each organization's journey will take a unique trajectory, reflecting a variety of current capabilities and business priorities. Still, several lessons can inform both first steps and larger leaps toward a redesign of work.

Capitalizing on What's Already Going On

In many firms, the proliferation of workplace options has unfolded in an uncoordinated fashion, without an overarching framework to provide clarity and maximize value. For example, when the National Science Foundation surveyed twelve hundred of its employees, it found that almost one-third teleworked regularly, and the number swelled to more than half when occasional teleworkers were counted. Not only that, but two-thirds of managers who supervised home-based workers also worked from home themselves.[44] All this was happening without a formal telework policy, illustrating how lattice ways to work are already occurring, albeit informally.

Similarly, a large pharmaceutical firm reviewed seven locations in expensive real estate markets, only to learn that average space utilization was a mere 41 percent. Many people were working out of the office at customer sites, at other offices, or at remote locations of their own choosing.[45] In this respect, employees' desire for flexibility—and the technology to achieve it—seems to be running ahead of the management mind-set to provide it. By waking up to what is already going on, organizations can take strides to reduce real estate expenses and improve workspace effectiveness. Formal policies and programs also help attract and retain talent, a benefit that under-the-radar arrangements can't deliver—as well as making access to options more equitable.

A good starting point is simply to look at how employees are currently performing their jobs, segmenting employee work patterns just as companies segment customer markets. How organizations go about this—whether they conduct surveys, organize focus groups, or formally observe workers—depends on available resources and the size of the effort. Whichever method (or combination of efforts) is chosen, a data-driven view is helpful in plotting the path forward.

Focusing on Work Effectiveness

By asking, "How can we be more effective?" teams naturally end up addressing how members want to grow and be challenged and how they want career and life to fit together. The advantage is that they tackle these topics through the lens of driving better business results and create a win-win for individuals and organizations.

The story of Xerox's work redesign illustrates the power of this focus. In the early 1990s, current chairman Anne Mulcahy was a line manager who wanted to see whether it was possible to advance a "dual agenda" of greater efficiency and effectiveness with greater integration of personal and professional life.[46] Xerox learned that the goals could be met if there was collective decision making at the team level about all three components—the where, when, and how—of work. As MIT professor Bailyn, who led a research team at Xerox, explains, "No longer was it possible for employees to negotiate for flexibilities one-on-one with their supervisors—since everyone now wanted some change—and the resulting necessity for collective negotiations at the work-unit level led supervisors away from continuous surveillance of their employees. It moved the division head toward a more open and innovative style of managing, and led to viewing flexibility as a collective opportunity for rethinking work effectiveness, rather than as a problem for individual employees and their supervisors."[47]

A team approach multiplies options, creating a wide range of choices to meet individual and organizational needs. For example, if one employee wants to start early and leave early and another wants to start late and leave late, these individual requests may present challenges for the business. In the context of a team, however, staggered schedules may actually increase effectiveness as they improve customers' access to employees for a longer period each day.

Given the move to team-based projects, more workers need what were previously management-level skills, such as facilitation or project planning. Companies can increase productivity by providing training in these critical competencies.

Measuring What Matters

Although the potential for improvements is great, reaping the benefits of workplace options requires changes in the ways people are managed and performance is measured. "Face time as a means to measure productivity of knowledge workers is becoming less and less relevant," says Pfizer's Clemons. "Even for more traditional industries—given globalization, access to information, and the greater independence of today's knowledge-worker roles—management-by-walking-around measures are being replaced with means that more accurately measure contributions, including accomplishments relative to goals and team feedback and results."[48]

Research confirms the validity of this approach. An academic study examined the influence of face time on performance evaluation and concluded that supervisors do have cognitive biases that can result in their giving higher ratings to those employees who are physically present than to those who are not. The authors conclude, "By showing that perceptions of employees at work are based on non-performance cues such as passive face time, without observers even being aware of the attributions they are making, the present study adds to the list of reasons not to use trait-based performance evaluation scales." They strongly recommend that companies adopt evaluation approaches that "explicitly consider employees' work output and contributions to corporate performance."[49]

Organizations that give individuals and managers leeway to decide when and where work gets done and align performance measurements to account for this increased autonomy enjoy great employee satisfaction and high performance. PNC Financial Services Group, the fifth-largest bank (based on deposits) in the United States, has found that allowing teams to customize schedules and work has heightened workers' understanding and accountability for the overall team goals and objectives.[50] Supporting a performance-based culture is yet another instance of how lattice organizations strengthen business performance.

It's All About Mind-Set

Lattice ways of working often challenge ladder-era beliefs. "In many organizations, time put in at the office is seen as a valid measure of commitment and competence," Bailyn says. "There can also be deep-seated beliefs about what is considered real work. And these beliefs often overemphasize technical tasks and under-emphasize relational tasks." She adds that another common challenge is the practice of never presenting a problem until someone has a solution: "Then people aren't concerned ever with preventing problems, but just with heroically solving problems, even if they cause them by themselves. These assumptions about very basic things get in the way of changing how work happens."[51]

Lattice ways to work often progress in fits and starts, with pockets of strength here and there. Sometimes technology leaps ahead of cultural change, and at other times it lags behind. The lack of adequate technology infrastructure and tools can be a serious problem in some companies, and employees are often vocal in their needs. Yet technology alone does not produce bottom-line benefits. Also critical is to modify attitudes and behaviors.

Frequently technology outpaces changes in the culture. The gap causes new technology investment results to fall short of a company's expectations. Citigroup, for example, had the technology to allow its people to work virtually, but only when it developed a cohesive, comprehensive approach that included management and performance expectations did the company realize the full power of remote working.[52]

Lattice ways to work are grounded firmly in benefits to the business *and* to the individual. They involve a realignment of the ground rules of the corporation so that work simply works bet-ter—for everyone. And just as expectations about the workplace must change, so too must the expectations of those who partici-pate in the life of the organization. As chapter 5 shows, participa-tion is based on high levels of collaboration and transparency, which starts at the individual level just as work does and over time spreads outward to teams and then to the entire culture.

5 ▶ LATTICE WAYS TO PARTICIPATE

Great discoveries and improvements invariably
involve the cooperation of many minds.

—*Alexander Graham Bell*

A S THE DEFINITION OF the workplace expands
from a physical and highly structured environment to a more virtual and highly adaptive
one, so too does the notion of how people participate in organizations and indeed in the greater world. The nature of work communication, relationships, knowledge, and value creation is changing,
becoming increasingly accessible and tailored to the ways each
person chooses to contribute. In lattice organizations, broader
participation means that people at all levels have options to share
ideas and grow knowledge, access critical information, and interact in communities and teams that span boundaries of all kinds.
Participation both relies on and creates a culture of inclusivity
that is not characteristic of ladder organizations.

This transformation of participation works in tandem with lattice ways to build careers and to get work done. It increases options for learning and growth, fosters innovation, enriches corporate culture, and boosts careers. As employees participate in broader company workings, they become better versed in organizational strategy, operations, and happenings and therefore contribute more and perform better than those who do not participate in this way. They also enjoy more active and engaged learning opportunities than the traditional one-way flow of information affords.

In the corporate ladder world, participation is generally tied to a person's physical location, department, and box on the organization chart. The higher your position and the closer you are to the head office, the more in-the-know you are on key decisions and the greater voice you have in shaping them. Internal communication cascades down the chain of command, and access to information is on a need-to-know basis. Social networks are fostered through in-person interactions at industry gatherings and at watercoolers. Information also flows up, ever so slowly, from rank-and-file workers in a sometimes filtered fashion. In many companies, the unspoken assumption is that those at the top are the only ones whose opinions are worthwhile.

In marked contrast, the lattice organization enables broad-based participation across levels and departmental boundaries. Relationships are more loosely coupled and not as strongly tied to hierarchy or location. An unprecedented amount of unfiltered information is accessible through formal and informal networks, often online. There are more avenues for building networks, gaining expertise, making distinctive contributions, and becoming known—the rock-solid links between participation and careers.

In flattening their structures, organizations have pushed down accountability and decision making to the front lines, so employees can provide real-time responses to customers and markets. Employees therefore have more knowledge and insight to contribute than used to be the case, and, with a greater voice, they are more engaged. People feel connected when a company communicates and collaborates with them in the multiple ways they use in their own increasingly networked lives.

THE TWIN FORCES OF PARTICIPATION

As we show in this chapter, the rules of participation are being reshaped—and in some cases, rewritten. Lattice organizations allow employees to customize how they voice their opinions, provide feedback, and collaborate—whether or not they choose to. New forms of contribution, in turn, challenge traditional relationships and communication. They create empowered workers and an inclusive work environment, at all levels in the hierarchy. We call these lattice ways to participate.

Examples abound of companies that employ the tenets of mass participation effectively in the marketplace. The results can be seen most easily in leading-edge Internet companies like Wikipedia, Amazon.com, Craigslist, Facebook, Twitter, LinkedIn, and Google, which rely on the contributions of millions of outsiders to power their services. But these are not the only ones. Many other types of companies are becoming skilled at tapping in to the power of the wisdom of the crowd, particularly the wisdom *inside* a company.

Lattice ways to participate harness two interrelated forces: collaboration and transparency. These forces are two sides of the same coin: each is distinctive enough to be considered separately, but in practice they are related aspects of one whole. Together, they describe the evolution in thinking and acting that is necessary to implement lattice styles of participation effectively (see table 5-1).

Lattice organizations realize that collaboration and transparency enhance the authenticity and effectiveness of internal and external communication—a critical ingredient for increasing employee engagement and productivity and ultimately burnishing

TABLE 5-1

A comparison of ladder and lattice thinking about participation

Ladder participation norms	Lattice participation norms
Top-down communication	Multidirectional communication
One-way, prescriptive instructions	Interactive group dialogue
Information shared with those who need to know	A variety of information available to those who need or want to know
Individual contribution	Community contribution
Hierarchical level determines how individuals contribute to the corporate agenda	Multiple, nonhierarchical options enable individual choice about how to contribute to the corporate agenda
Command and control	Collaboration and influence
Limited transparency inhibits trust	Transparency encourages trust

a company's talent brand. As information flows broaden, the importance of brand and reputation for individuals and organizations grows, because brands provide a shortcut through information overload. As you saw in chapter 1, there is intensifying competition to earn coveted best-places-to-work awards and rankings, and an industry is emerging to help companies improve their practices and ultimately their brands.

A company's brand is what the marketplace perceives it to be. Employees, former employees, suppliers, customers, and shareholders are among the influencers who now have their own forums to shape a brand as they interact with each other, sometimes inside and sometimes outside the four walls of the organization. As expectations grow for ways to participate, a company's failure to embrace and harness these sources of reputational power can create a chasm between employee expectations and their work experiences, and ultimately fuel a horde of brand dissenters.

Greater collaboration and transparency inside a firm, on the other hand, can result in a greater sense of community and pride in the organization, creating a cadre of brand ambassadors. Both realities signal that brands everywhere—including talent brands—depend on what people really think and feel about an organization.

The Collaboration Economy

The word *collaboration* is derived from the Latin *collaborare,* which means "to labor together." Given the ever-increasing pace of global business, laboring together collaboratively becomes critical to keeping pace. Rather than focus on defending a few key ideas, or "stocks of knowledge," companies must use "flows of knowledge" to continuously generate newer and better ideas.[1]

Collaboration is a means of tapping in to the flow of information, knowledge, and teamwork across internal and extended organizational networks. In many companies, a cross section of colleagues from different levels comes together both in person and virtually to collaborate, share interests, connect, create, and innovate. Communities of practice and other networks, often self-forming, coalesce around the skills and experiences that people have in common. Because there are many networks and ways to participate in them, social and learning experiences become customized to the individual.

Procter & Gamble (P&G), for example, has set up communities of practice to bolster its innovation strategy.[2] Within research and development alone, it has established more than twenty communities, bringing together people from disciplines such as packaging, skin care, and fragrance.[3] The communities help share expertise across the company. Experts from its flavored coffee producers and other P&G brands, in one instance, helped craft new flavors of Crest toothpaste.[4] The goals of the P&G communities typify what communities of practice are all about: building the technical excellence of members, solving difficult challenges, and cross-pollinating organizational knowledge faster than prior approaches. In addition to benefiting the development of a wide range of products, these communities help individuals grow and develop. P&G even highlights them in its recruiting brochure for doctoral students.[5]

At the U.S. Government Accountability Office (GAO), communities of practice first formed about five years ago to cultivate the specialized expertise needed to fulfill the agency's mission and to, as former Chief Learning Officer Carol Willett explains, "tap in to the power of peer learning and peer collaboration."[6] These early communities brought people together but struggled to capture and share knowledge at scale.

Enter the GAO wiki, a collaboratively written content resource that was rolled out in 2008. Spanning the agency's twelve locations, the wiki offered a rapid way to solicit contributions from those who couldn't always be present at meetings. In fairly short order, communities evolved to help connect experts with organization needs. "In a very positive way, the technology is being hijacked by people and being put to very good purposes, and they're using the technology in pursuit of finding the expertise that is going to enable them to contribute more effectively and thereby enhance their careers," says Willett.

As the GAO's story illustrates, social technologies that help people interact and share information make it dramatically easier to find people to collaborate with, in turn making work more effective and efficient. A recent survey concluded that three-fourths of executives say they plan to maintain or increase investments in networking and related technologies that encourage internal collaboration. Nearly half use or plan to use Web 2.0 tools to foster collective intelligence and peer-to-peer networking, and one-third use online social networks, blogs, RSS, podcasts, and wikis.[7]

As workers increasingly connect with their coworkers through the same social networks they use every day in their personal lives, personal and professional networks are beginning to blend. And as younger generations gravitate toward massively multiplayer online role-playing games for entertainment, such as the

12-million-strong community that plays World of Warcraft (WoW), they are simultaneously looking for the same "multiplayer" experience in the e-learning and other development opportunities their companies provide. Changing expectations mean that companies must construct development and collaboration opportunities online that are just as engaging as the worlds employees already inhabit. Venture capitalist and WoW participant Joi Ito says that "what we are doing in WoW represents in many ways the future of real time collaborative teams and leadership in an increasingly ad hoc, always-on, diversity-intense, and real-time environment."[8]

The greater the level of collaboration created through these and other methods, the greater the sense of belonging and the greater the ownership in the result. Studies have shown that teamwork and collaboration within and between groups can predict an organization's shareholder value and long-term employee productivity, effectiveness, and retention.[9] What's more, 87 percent of highly engaged employees believe that their companies do a good job of encouraging the sharing of information and ideas across the company, compared with 10 percent of employees with low engagement.[10]

And collaboration inside and outside a company is vital to providing career-enhancing experiences that develop talent. "Talented workers join companies and stay there because they believe they'll learn faster and better than they would at other employers," say authors John Hagel and John Seely Brown.[11] "They get better, faster by trying new things, by experimenting with what they do in their jobs and how they do it, and by tackling real problems with other talented people with different backgrounds and skills—people who are just as likely to work for other companies, in other locales, as they are to be working in the same company."

Career-enhancing organizations, which we explore in chapter 3, foster the continual learning of market-relevant skills that employees prize. When knowledge workers get better and faster, they are more engaged and also learn better, forming a virtuous cycle of development and performance. "Learning and development is a social process, and engagement, through participation and other means, is a facilitator of learning," says Maryam Alavi, vice dean of the Goizueta Business School at Emory University.[12]

There is also a connection between collaboration and an inclusive workplace that is not divided along gender, generational, cultural, or ethnic lines. In a heterogeneous marketplace, a diversity of thoughts, backgrounds, and experiences increases the value of the new products and services that result from collaboration, because they are informed by a greater understanding of the customer. "Among service providers, clients often select someone with whom they have things in common," says Bob Bertagna, senior managing director and head of industrials at Macquarie Capital. "Tapping in to the best and the brightest, as the workforce becomes more diverse, means expanding the type of people that we've historically recruited and providing an environment where they can prosper."[13]

Pfizer is tapping in to its network of diversity affinity groups to drive participation in its broader business agenda. Groups for women, minorities, and gays and lesbians, for example, are encouraged to collaborate on target marketing strategies to those groups and to assist with ensuring there is ample diversity in the makeup of clinical trials. "We're trying to find that sweet spot between taking advantage of the amazing amount of energy our colleagues are bringing to work every day and their desire to contribute, while at the same time not making them feel as though there's one right way to participate that corporate dictates," says Tanya Clemons.[14]

Moreover, companies that can tap in to the power of diversity make better decisions. The more complex the business challenge, in fact, the more you want a heterogeneous group of people working together to tackle it. Scott Page, an economist and professor of complex systems at the University of Michigan, has built mathematical models for all sorts of systems that are highly interrelated and complex, including diverse teams. He found that the more wide ranging the backgrounds, the better the problem-solving ability, as long as each member of the group collaborates and brings his unique experience and perspective to the table.[15]

The payoff for getting collaboration right is big. Not only do collective know-how and decision making generate measurable improvements in a company's products, services, and work processes, but they also create an organizational environment that is diverse, engaging, and therefore productive. It expands the pool of potential team members and taps in to a range of insights.

That's what AT&T is experiencing with one of its social media experiments. John Donovan, AT&T's chief technology officer, was looking for a nonhierarchical approach to harness the rich depth of knowledge and creativity inside the multibillion-dollar firm.[16] Leveraging social media, Donovan created a mass participation approach to innovation that, by design, would not replicate the company's existing functional or hierarchical organizational structure.

This approach features a Web site that allows anyone (and Donovan is quick to underscore *anyone*) to contribute an idea, become a collaborator on someone else's idea, provide encouragement and critical feedback, assess a concept's marketability, challenge its engineering and affordability, and the like. Each employee can also vote on the caliber of the insights and rate additional postings of suggestions and comments, earning the contributors reputation points. "This is meritocracy at its best—a highly diverse set of people, in every sense of the word, crowd-sourcing and crowd-storming," says Donovan. (*Crowd-storming* is brainstorming using a large, virtual group.)

The beauty of the tactic is manifold. Individuals can customize their level of participation—from merely being a spectator to actively participating and racking up reputation points. The system self-polices. And, as Donovan says, "In an *American Idol*—type

The Benefits of Collaboration

- Improves effectiveness and efficiency

- Enables better teamwork

- Improves the quality of decisions through an inclusive culture

- Stimulates innovation

- Retains talent by strengthening connections and a sense of belonging

- Cultivates networks and provides options for learning, expanding career–life choices

fashion, unknown talent is revealed and great innovations can see the light of day."

Season 1 netted about six hundred ideas and eighty-five hundred active participants, and the site has grown from one hundred to five hundred new participants per day. Such results are a strong measure of participation's role in generating recognition for individuals and engagement in the business overall. By the end of its third quarter, the site had more than twenty-four thousand members, two thousand ideas, and more than a million page views and was still growing.[17] The first season's winners have been funded and are moving from PowerPoint to prototype.

The less formally structured and more nimble lattice world also highlights a necessary core competency: the need to align the silos of the organization and get the people within them to work together. How can you make sure that groups are working together well, particularly given the high levels of diversity across lines of geography, background, expertise, and roles? These are table-stakes skills in today's workplace.

The "Through the Looking Glass" Organization

In addition to building collaborative systems of participation, companies are growing more transparent—easier to see into and out of. Transparency transcends the boundaries of the corporation. In fact, transparency *outside* the organization is driving the transparency agenda internally—and at an unprecedented level.

Now, anyone can access online information that previously was shared only on a need-to-know basis. Web sites such as Vault.com, Salary.com, and Glassdoor.com let employees anonymously share salaries and the inside scoop on what it is like to work for a firm. Employees and competitors alike can also learn about once closely held developments through sites that studiously follow a company's every move. And employees communicate with each other and those outside the company more than ever before through Web 2.0 technologies.

The 92-million-member Millennial generation has been raised with the tools of transparency, and they are as natural to Gen Yers as the air they breathe. Younger generations *expect* open access to information. As Clive Thompson wrote in *Wired*, "A generation has grown up blogging, posting a daily phone cam picture on Flickr, and listing its geographic position in real time on [services such as] Google Maps. For them, authenticity comes from online exposure. It's hard to trust anyone who *doesn't* list their dreams and fears on Facebook."[18] Boomers, too, see the value of deeply participatory and transparent technologies. More than 60 percent of Boomers are avid consumers of social media such as blogs, forums, podcasts, and online videos, according to Forrester Research.[19]

Hallmarks of participation include the amount of information and the variety of methods to communicate it as well as the transparent flow of information in multiple directions throughout the lattice organization. Indeed, the flattening of org-chart hierarchies now extends to the flattening of communication hierarchies. From user-rating systems to "how helpful was this information?"

buttons, quick "pulse surveys," comments on blog postings, and online voting, people have more opportunities than ever before to weigh in. Companies can no longer broadcast their opinions one-way and leave it at that. Their workers are broadcasting back, as well as back and forth with each other.

Transparency also shines a spotlight on a firm's weakest links. Uncensored employee postings have the clear potential for embarrassing disclosures, serious damage to a company's brand, and loss of valuable information assets. Companies today are compelled to address issues and perceptions that in the past might have stayed in the shadows. Indeed, 74 percent of employed Americans participating in a Deloitte *Workplace and Ethics Survey* in 2009 believe activity on popular social networking sites can easily damage a company's reputation.[20] The new house of business is indeed built of glass.

For example, United Airlines endured a public relations tsunami in the summer of 2009 when a disgruntled customer felt that he was poorly treated after his checked guitar was damaged during baggage handling. Rather than continue to argue with the airline over who was responsible, David Carroll wrote, recorded, and uploaded a music video titled "United Breaks Guitars" to YouTube. As of December 2009 the video had garnered more than 6 million hits, more than 23,000 comments, and even a visit to the *Today* show for Carroll.[21] Things wound up working out well for him and his band: United offered to pay for the damage (which he refused), and his "United" single sold briskly on iTunes.

Lattice organizations understand that although online chatter may be incomplete, taken out of context, or flat wrong, such unofficial sources are important channels through which people get and contribute information. These media therefore warrant attention. According to the Workplace & Ethics survey, only 17 percent of executives reported that their companies have monitoring mechanisms and mitigation plans in place for social media.[22] Smart companies recognize the importance of authentic and transparent communications to develop credibility in these channels and to build relationships of influence.

Lattice firms also mix it up, providing varied communication channels that align with the number of ways heterogeneous workers prefer to connect and to receive and respond to information. Best Buy, for example, now has many avenues for dialogue that transcend hierarchy. The *Fortune* 100 consumer electronics retailer of everything from flat-screen TVs and home appliances to cell phones and laptops has transformed how it communicates with employees to be transparent and inclusive. Jennifer Rock, Best Buy's director of employee communications, explains: "Most companies traditionally communicate at employees. They send a message to employees and the message gets received, you hope, and now we're done. But that's not how the world works anymore. Internal communications is moving from a role of being the ones who own the messages and deliver them to employees to a role that we are just facilitators. We're encouraging, we're enabling."[23]

One of its first steps to more open communications was Blue Shirt Nation, an internal social networking site that encourages employees to share and discuss their unfiltered customer service experiences and ideas for improvements. Steve Bendt and Gary Koelling, two junior corporate marketing employees launched the site in 2006 with no corporate IT support or funding on an extra server stashed under one of their desks. Now more than twenty-five thousand employees use Blue Shirt Nation each month to communicate and solve problems.[24]

The retailer has found that information delivered via employees through the intranet is more effective than any company memo. The site ran a contest to spur employees to contribute to their 401(k) plans; workers submitted videos they had conceived and produced with no company oversight. The contest resulted in a 30 percent increase in plan enrollment. And an employee revolt on Blue Shirt Nation led the company to reverse a plan to change the popular employee discount. The site has also led associates to solve mundane problems, such as a too-tall camera display case, in a few days as opposed to the weeks it normally would have taken to wind through the corporate bureaucracy.[25] These results demonstrate that transparent communication at the ground level leads to employee empowerment, commitment, and engagement.

The experiment has led to other efforts, including a wiki, an innovation space called The Loop, and TagTrade, a prediction market where employees are encouraged to make their projections on everything from product trends to the success of new services.[26] Three years ago, an executive sparked the site by asking hundreds of employees to predict the number of Best Buy gift cards the company would sell in a month. The collective wisdom of employees wound up being closer to the actual number than the forecast executives had calculated.

Best Buy is not alone. Nearly four-fifths of responding companies in a recent survey report that they use social technologies frequently to engage employees and foster productivity, outranking even e-mail. Company blogs are the most popular, with 47 percent of businesses using them.[27]

Innovative methods of generating transparency are important tactics in the race for employee engagement. No matter how it's achieved, information sharing has measurable benefits. According to Watson Wyatt, 90 percent of highly engaged workers say their immediate supervisor keeps them informed about management decisions, as compared with 24 percent of low-engagement workers. And 85 percent of highly engaged employees say their company does a good job of seeking the opinions and suggestions of employees, as compared with 7 percent of low-engagement employees.[28]

The 2008 "World of Work" employee survey conducted by Randstad and Harris Interactive found that more than half of employees think it is important that employers seek their "honest input on business issues," placing the issue among the top 10 for creating what the survey calls "employership." But only a quarter of the same employees saw this trait in their company, creating a gap between hopes and reality.[29] As you saw in chapter 3, these gaps can show up in bright lights in the ubiquitous best-places-to-work rankings.

Transparency motivates employees because it fosters trust. According to a report from Development Dimensions International, "Trust means employees have confidence that others' actions are consistent with their words, that leadership is concerned about their welfare and interests apart from what they can do for the organization, that the skills they have developed are respected and valued, and that each employee uniquely matters in the workplace."[30]

Studies show that trust is a critical success factor in organizational performance.[31] According to one survey, total return to shareholders over a three-year period was 186 percent higher for those companies that had high levels of trust compared with those that had lower levels of trust.[32] It is no coincidence that the *Fortune* 100 Best Companies to Work For ranking is based on a survey that includes a "trust index." Transparency is the secret sauce that engenders trust.

Why Transparency Matters

- Strengthens authenticity of talent brand

- Improves organizational effectiveness

- Reduces the cycle time to identify issues and react to opportunities

- Raises performance by building trust, a key enabler of effective organizations

ADVANCING LATTICE WAYS OF PARTICIPATING

Ways to participate are constantly emerging and changing, but a number of leading organizations are learning important lessons along the way. Here are some of the most salient.

Let Many Experiments Bloom

Intuit cofounder and Executive Committee chairman Scott Cook has coined the term *user-contribution systems* to describe the new forms of mass participation we have explored in this chapter.[33] The systems allow customers, employees, and sales prospects—or even people with no previous connection to a company—to actively or passively contribute work, expertise, information, or behavioral data to a site that aggregates and automatically converts it into something useful to others, with little or no intervention by an organization.

Intuit learned important lessons from its own efforts to deploy user-contribution systems for mass participation. The Silicon Valley firm, which has eighty-two hundred employees and $3.1 billion in revenues, provides financial software and Web services to consumers, small- to mid-size businesses, financial institutions, and accounting professionals. As Cook readily admits, the notion that people were willing to help his company create value for customers and shareholders *for free* struck him as "unfathomable."

Intuit began with a small-scale experiment, creating the free TaxAlmanac forum and wiki, where tax preparers can raise (and answer) often obscure questions. More than 400,000 tax professionals flooded the online space to contribute questions and answers for the benefit of other tax preparers in the Intuit community. The site also has served as an excellent opportunity for Intuit to acquire new customers at little cost.

"It's about getting out of the conference rooms and actively experimenting," says Cook. He recommends that companies model many small experiments and then get rapid feedback from customers, employees, and stakeholders.[34] Noting that CEOs sometimes fail to properly predict the impact of new products, Cook says that the role of a leader is not to make every decision about the company's future but instead to create a "culture of experimentation" wherein customers' votes on small experiments are used to figure out what works.[35]

Bring Outside Thinking Inside

From Intuit's many experiments, it has learned that user contributions depend on customers' sharing their thoughts or knowledge in ways that are meaningful or interesting to them. Or as Cook puts it, "They participate simply to be recognized."[36]

This is precisely what editors of the *Economist* realized when they launched an online capability to comment on articles posted to Economist.com. Even though on average the weekly print edition contains fifteen times as many words as the online edition, the Web site now receives many times the volume of letters to the editor as the print version typically does. Explains Ben Edwards, publisher and executive vice president of Economist.com, "We learned that our readers want to contribute to the dialogue, to give feedback, to express their own opinions and/or experience on any given topic, and that they will take the time to do so particularly when it's invited and made easy to do so." And from the *Economist*'s point of view, the more time readers are engaged with it, the less time they are spending with competitors' publications.[37]

Individuals are finding innovative means to participate outside the office and in the process are upending traditional notions of what happens both inside and outside the company's four walls. Health care providers, entrepreneurs, and corporations, for example, are providing consumers with Web 2.0 methods that enable patients to become partners in their own care, a significant change in thinking for a top-down, expert-driven industry. For instance, the online social network PatientsLikeMe has banded together more than twenty-three thousand critically ill patients—having such chronic illnesses as amyotrophic lateral sclerosis (ALS), multiple sclerosis, Parkinson's disease, HIV/AIDS, fibromyalgia, and mood disorders—who chart their symptoms and treatment results in minute detail on the site. The hope is that the information will help researchers and patients alike learn what's working to help better manage disease symptoms in the short run and ultimately develop cures. The founders describe the site as a "treatment-, symptom-, and outcome-sharing community."[38]

It's clear that an increased ability to participate is seeping into our personal lives—and smart companies are extending it to the workplace to forge new paths to participation and foster inclusiveness of employees at all levels and backgrounds. This ability to participate motivates people through a strong sense of belonging, an enriched sense of pride in their contributions, and a high level of satisfaction in having a positive reputation in the community.

Evolutionary, Not Revolutionary

Most organizations are already experiencing forms of mass participation that they can build on. Experiments are often blooming, with or without leaders' engagement.

Similar to a turbine taking advantage of the wind, a lattice organization capitalizes on what is naturally occurring to create greater levels of energy. It understands that by embracing new means of broad participation, work is ultimately more engaging for all. As employees see the results of their participation, they also become more knowledgeable, insightful, and engaged—driving productivity and innovation.

Companies can start by taking stock of current efforts and figuring out the value each is creating—and how to capture more value from them. To help gauge the state of your company's approach, see figure 5-1, which depicts the stages of advancement along the participation journey. It provides benchmarks to aid you in assessing where you are and where you might go next. You might even consider how you can institutionalize, customize, and integrate what's already going on to deliver strategic value, as AT&T, Best Buy, and Intuit have done.

A prime example of a company moving toward the higher end of lattice ways to participate is British telecommunications giant BT. The company's social media efforts began about three years ago with a wiki called BTpedia, which facilitates information sharing across the company. Initially, BTpedia operated on a server that sat under the desk of a recent college graduate who connected the software to the intranet. Few people understood it at first. At this point, BT was at the low-level expression depicted in figure 5-1, with initial experiments using disconnected "cool" tools.

Having spent decades as a collection of government-operated organizations, BT was privatized in 1984 and during the following years transformed itself from a traditional, monopolistic, and hierarchical civil-service corporation. Over the past decade, it has

FIGURE 5-1

The stages of lattice ways to participate

Low-level expression		High-level expression
Reactionary, usually in response to grassroots activity, with little strategic focus or intent	Generally proactive, although opportunistic and discrete	Proactively designed as a portfolio of strategic ways to connect and tap into an important organizational asset

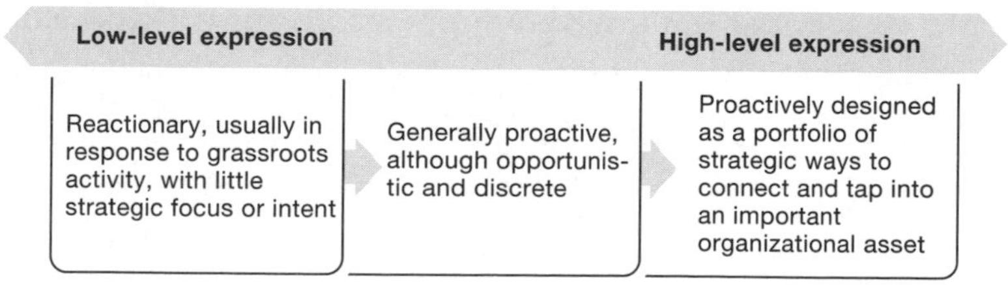

removed several layers from its hierarchy, becoming a "much flatter, free-flowing organization where what matters is what you know," says Richard Dennison, currently principal business partner at BT and formerly a senior manager of social media.[39] "It's much more about having a set of skills, building up a kind of reputation, and then people tapping in to those skills."

As BTpedia built momentum, a second experiment was launched to introduce blogging, and a third soon followed that created a small-scale social network. At this point, the ad hoc effort hit a wall when the server—still under an employee's desk—couldn't carry the load of three enterprise applications. The IT department was subsequently engaged and helped design a robust internal social network called My BT. The network has Facebook-like functionality that lets individuals customize their own pages, something that was unusual in the corporate environment at the time.

My BT is designed with the high degree of integration that characterizes advanced expressions of participation. It provides one-stop shopping to access the content an employee has created on BTpedia, in blogs, and elsewhere. It also shows what other colleagues in a network are up to. This integrated approach was a hit. People quickly "got it," says Dennison. "They could suddenly see what the point of this whole social media exercise was, which was linking together with like-minded people, being updated with what they were working on, being able to see activity and connect with new people. It created a bigger picture, which I think helped people get the whole point of social media."

BT's customized and integrated approach is currently developing toward high-end expression. Its efforts now proactively target strategic outcomes such as innovation. "I don't think that you can have an innovative company unless every single employee thinks they can make a difference to the organization," says Dennison. "These tools are a key enabler for people to think they can make a difference."

Make Participation "Simply Part of How Business Is Done"

Eventually, collaboration and transparency become part of the playbook that everyone follows. For example, Goldman Sachs has institutionalized a 360-degree review system that quantitatively analyzes feedback from a wide range of colleagues—what people think of your trading results, the deals you have done, the projects you have led or contributed to, and so on. It also solicits and factors in feedback from geographic and functional perspectives. What do your global colleagues think about your performance? What do your core team members think? The continual learning provided by this feedback is an important way Goldman delivers a career-enhancing experience to employees.

And when individuals improve their performance, the company's performance improves too. Edith Hunt, COO of human capital management and head of global recruiting at Goldman Sachs, reports that "this form of transparency yields very high participation from the top of the organization on through." Some 96 percent of Goldman Sachs colleagues write reviews when requested, and then managers sit with each team member to review the feedback. "Yes, even our chairman and chief executive officer, Lloyd Blankfein, receives 360-degree feedback," Hunt says.[40] Such a nonhierarchical stance underlies the transparency that is essential to advancing lattice participation.

Trust Begets Trust

Companies are often understandably concerned about having appropriate risk management processes in place, particularly as collaboration and communication become interactive, transparent, and community driven. BT learned early on, however, that employees care about the company and their own personal reputations, and these are powerful motivators of appropriate intra-organizational social network conduct. And the rules become self-reinforcing.

"It just doesn't make sense to me that just because you give somebody something that they can abuse, that they are going to abuse it," says BT's Dennison. "People care about what other people think of them."[41] BT mitigates this risk by offering clear guidelines about what people can and can't discuss as well as editorial guidelines that cover such topics as tone of voice and not posting when you're angry. BT engaged HR and other policy-making areas early on; provided brief, common sense guidance; and rolled out a process for users to report inappropriate content.

The efforts have paid off. Despite being in a highly regulated industry with specific restrictions on information that cannot be shared across the enterprise, BT hasn't experienced any violations of its policies thus far. Lattice participation has become embedded in how work is done.

Lattice organizations widen their views of whose voices can make a difference and where good ideas can come from. They acknowledge they are living in a house of glass and become less controlling and more candid and interactive in their communication. Leveraging new technologies, company employees become connectors of all the moving parts of the business as they never could before. And organizations enable greater customization of communication and contributions and therefore increase their personal relevance. The combination helps lattice ways to participate proliferate throughout the company.

———————

Participation is the third and last of the three lattice ways we explore in this book. When they are integrated and fueled with greater customization, the power of each lattice way is amplified, as you will see in three detailed case studies we turn to next.

6 ▶ LATTICE JOURNEYS

*It is not a question of how well each process works.
The question is how well they all work together.*

—*Lloyd Dobens*

AS WE HAVE EXPLORED throughout this book, industrial age ladder hierarchies are giving way to the modern structure of the lattice. To be sure, lattice organizations continue to feature vertical hierarchies on their organization charts, but these structures are flatter and less rigid, with more matrixed reporting lines and more expansive flows of information, communication, and relationships. They are overlaid with a horizontal scaffolding of sorts—an adaptive architecture for careers, work, and participation.

In previous chapters we discussed the converging trends that influence lattice realities, and we examined many facets of the lattice individually. We now explore how companies put the lattice into practice—in particular, how the three lattice ways mesh and how each reinforces the others. An initial move into one area, as you will see, often prompts or strengthens a change elsewhere. As

TABLE 6-1

Connections between the lattice ways

	Careers	Work	Participation
Careers		Changes to work and careers propel a shift toward results and away from face time.	New forms of participation offer more options to learn, build relationships, and build personal brands.
Work	Career–life options expand along with anytime, anywhere work options.		Virtual collaboration and networks enable redesigned work processes.
Participation	Transparency enables more candor about career options and how they fit with life choices.	Work increasingly relies on flexible teams that need to collaborate transparently.	

these efforts interconnect, the lattice organization takes visible shape. Table 6-1 describes these connections.

In this chapter we focus on three organizations—Cisco, Deloitte LLP, and Thomson Reuters—that are far along on their journeys toward lattice living. On the surface these companies appear to have little in common—they represent different industries and offer diverse products and services—but they share distinctively lattice ways of thinking and acting, and they demonstrate lattice-fueled results.

None of the companies specifically set out to respond to the underlying shift from ladder to lattice, but leaders in each company intuitively sensed the changing landscape and have been successful in reinventing their organizations in response. And their approaches are consistent with a key theme throughout this book—that the evolution to the lattice is already going on.

These firms' transformations are by no means complete, but their progress illuminates the road ahead. Through these studies, the panorama of lattice living comes into focus.

LATTICE LIVING AT CISCO

Cisco was an exemplar of the dot-com boom, bust, and recovery cycle. Between 1993 and 2000, it acquired more than seventy technology companies, and in the process it grew into a computer-networking behemoth with a market capitalization of $579 billion—the highest of any firm in the world, eclipsing even Microsoft and GE.[1] But by September 2001, Cisco's stock had fallen 86 percent; it had laid off almost 20 percent of its workforce; and it had to take a record $2.2 billion inventory write-down as the Internet bubble burst and networking equipment piled up in warehouses.[2]

CEO John Chambers became a fervent believer in reinventing the company. Cisco began to evolve from a go-go growth culture to one based on teamwork, accountability, and productivity. It became more lattice-like not only in its culture but also in its structure.

Cisco now has a system of councils and boards to facilitate horizontal collaboration across what had been relatively siloed organizational areas. Social media and other technologies have been widely adopted to increase collaboration and efficiency in facing off with the marketplace. A new model for developing careers has also emerged—one that emphasizes lateral as well as vertical moves to grow high-potential, next-generation leaders. And options for integrating career and life have expanded as flexible work becomes the norm. These efforts showcase how being a lattice-in-action organization contributes to remarkable results.

Cisco emerged from the recession of the early 2000s more profitable than ever, and it is now one of the top one hundred largest companies in the world in market capitalization and revenue. At last count it had accumulated more than $35 billion in cash—a strategic asset and one of the biggest hoards in the technology world.[3] Not only have Cisco's lattice-style moves netted it sustained financial success, but also the company is now known as an employer of choice, as demonstrated by its top-ten ranking on the *Fortune* 100 Best Companies to Work For and *DiversityInc* Top 10 Global Diversity Companies, as well as rankings in *Working Mother* 100 Best Companies and *BusinessWeek*'s Best Places to Launch a Career.[4]

From Me to We

The cornerstone of Cisco's transformation was its move from an individualistic culture to one based on teamwork and collaboration—which together lie at the heart of lattice ways to work and participate. In 2002, Cisco implemented the first version of what would grow into a system of cross-functional councils and boards designed to pursue opportunities in specific areas and drive business performance horizontally across the company.

The structure was designed to both speed up the company's responsiveness to market conditions and push down decision making to lower levels than had previously existed at Cisco. "If you look at how most companies are organized, they are built around an informational discontinuity, where just a few people at the top are presumed to have access to vast amounts of knowledge," says Brian Schipper, senior vice president of human resources. "In a world where most people can access information about any subject in less than five minutes, this notion is outdated."[5]

As in most major efforts, points of view were argued adamantly, bet-the-farm decisions were made, and tough lessons were learned. "We discovered collaboration was different enough from how we used to operate that it wasn't enough to just put good leaders on the councils," says Randy Pond, executive vice president of operations, systems, and processes. "We needed to shift our cultural mind-set and provide more structure to support this change."[6]

So Cisco created a "taxonomy" for councils, defining a process for developing a vision, a strategy, and an execution plan for each. It stressed mutual accountability and teamwork and ensured that those on the councils could really speak for their areas of the company and commit to decisions. To make sure that this shift was given the needed focus and commitment, Chambers also announced that 30 percent of senior executives' bonuses would be based on how well they collaborated with others, a structural change in the reward system designed to support the larger cultural change already going on.[7]

As the approach evolved, Cisco found that it needed to match the governing mechanism with the size of the market. Councils are now set up for major business initiatives and multibillion-dollar market opportunities, whereas boards make the call on smaller-scale efforts. Working groups take on specific tasks in support of a council or board. This arrangement improves execution and enables an efficient division of labor; the working groups dissolve after their work is completed.

A few years in, the culture began to change. "We really started to see the benefit after our initial improvements," says Pond.[8] "We were starting to cross-pollinate knowledge and appropriately drive broader thinking. We began to get a relevant marketing comment out of the manufacturing guy or a supply-chain comment out of an engineering person."

The councils and boards are expanding leaders' capabilities, too. "People have opportunities for natural leadership and development in ways that we couldn't provide before," says Susan Monaghan, vice president of employee engagement. "Through experience, we are changing the way people lead. People are learning something that they can never unlearn. Over time, this changes the face of the culture."[9]

By late 2008, Cisco was using its council-based decision-making structure to handle twenty-two corporation-wide, cross-functional priorities. And its shifts in cultural and operating behaviors were netting financial results. For example, Cisco vice president Ron Ricci organized a board of fifteen sports fanatics with relevant skills to guide the company's entry into the sports business. Without the CEO's involvement, a multimillion-dollar business came together in fewer than 120 days, winning contracts with sports organizations such as the New York Yankees and the Dallas Cowboys. In fiscal 2008, Ricci saw the number of new projects increase tenfold while operating expenses were trimmed 2 to 3 percent. "We are doing all this at the vice-president and director level," says Ricci. "We don't need John [Chambers] to do this now."[10]

And Chambers agrees. Efforts to transform work and participation have made it possible for him to take himself out of the picture on many decisions. Cisco's move toward a participatory, nonhierarchical approach is based on what Chambers calls "co-labor" and the "collaboration marketplace."[11] The goal has been to spread decision making far wider to working groups that involve five hundred executives, helping the organization pursue a greater number of market opportunities than a more traditional command-and-control structure, says Don Proctor, senior vice president of software at Cisco.[12] The strategy also enhances succession planning. Chambers wants to transform the nature of the corporation itself, starting at the top: "You won't have to depend on the CEO anymore," he says. "We now have a whole pool of talent who can lead these working groups like mini CEOs and COOs. We're growing ideas, but we're growing people as well. Where I might have had two potential successors, I now have 500."[13]

The speed of decision making has also increased. "I think when people envision collaborative models, they picture a bunch of people endlessly trying to resolve problems in lieu of clarity and decisiveness that comes from hierarchy," explains Schipper. "But what gets missed in the equation is that the most precious commodity in most companies is senior leadership time. A council or a board that has all functions with a seat at the table doesn't need to wait the weeks or months to seek approval from another governing group with an already packed agenda. We move seamlessly from strategy to execution. Councils and boards dramatically accelerate the pace at which we are able to do things."[14]

The change was radical and in places tumultuous, resulting in about 20 percent of senior staff leaving the firm.[15] Two former executives say that Cisco's council-based approach allows Chambers to consolidate power by spreading potential rivals' authority widely across committees.[16] But Chambers disagrees, saying that the transition was well worth the effort. "When you have command and control by the top 10 people, you can only do one or two things at a time," he told *BusinessWeek*.[17]

Schipper weighs in, noting that "one of the biggest barriers to effective collaboration is a senior leadership team that is unwilling to cede control. That's usually because these leaders have not built the capability in their organizations for gaining alignment on vision and strategy. Without fundamentally changing leadership and governance practices to support collaboration, the benefits of accelerated results are unlikely to be realized."[18] Chambers sums up: "The future is about collaboration and teamwork and making decisions with a replicable process that offers scale, speed, and flexibility."[19]

Lattice Leadership Development

As collaboration through councils and boards became the management norm, Cisco realized it also needed to develop leadership talent differently. It had to evolve the traditional trajectories of executive careers to align with its new model. The revised effort focuses on the next generation of leadership, who ultimately will run a company that works very differently. Cisco is moving high-potential executives laterally as well as vertically to build the breadth of business perspectives that collaboration requires.

Consider the story of Ana Corrales, vice president of global business operations.[20] She joined Cisco in 1996 as a manufacturing planner to leverage her expertise in operations research. She then made a series of horizontal moves that gave her a broad portfolio of experience. "Early on in my career I didn't realize how valuable moving around the organization would be," says Corrales. "Cisco leaders and mentors really encouraged and pushed me to new roles." Corrales's move to manufacturing plant operations director netted her people leadership skills to add to her already formidable analytical strengths. Additional moves took her to materials procurement, to finance, and to customer service. "As a result of these experiences, when Ana talks about our business, she really understands how all the pieces work together," says Randy Pond.[21] "Today she is a vice president in charge of business models, a great new role we just created that requires a cross-functional perspective. This is the model for our future leaders."

As Corrales's experience illustrates, Cisco engineers custom development paths for its high-potential employees that include lateral moves to build future skills. Top leaders now conduct an annual review identifying who is ready to move and which positions would most benefit the individual and the organization.

To make its model scalable and repeatable, Cisco learned that it needed to teach leaders how to talk about career growth and development in more individualized ways. It created a set of leadership competencies to align with the new way of doing things and embedded them in the company's performance management process. Called C-LEAD (the acronym summarizes five key actions: collaborate, learn, execute, accelerate, and disrupt), the leadership competencies provide a common language for manager–employee conversations. The system pushes hard to make sure that personalized career conversations effectively discuss career interests and explore potential moves, both vertical and horizontal.

Rethinking the Workspace

Cisco's focus wasn't limited to executive levels. To improve employee productivity and broaden collaboration throughout the organization, in 2003 it began introducing what it calls the collaborative, connected workplace. Cisco set ambitious goals to improve productivity more than 10 percent per year for five years so that it could grow without having to hire a commensurate number of people.[22] One objective was to increase the number of employees without proportionately increasing real estate costs. Another was to create a more productive environment than traditional, cubicle-laden floor plans provided. All employees—and not only those with executive titles—would have a greater ability to customize how they accomplished work through a broad choice of workspaces and virtual work options.

Cisco employees, like those at many companies, are increasingly mobile, with fewer than 60 percent working at a permanently assigned desk. The company had previously designed its office space under the traditional ladder assumption that employees would sit at their own desks during regular work hours. The result was that meeting rooms were often in short supply, whereas offices and cubicles remained vacant 65 percent of the time, on average.[23]

The redesign of the physical offices features informal spaces with wheeled seating, mobile tables, and movable privacy screens that enable employees to spontaneously create a collaborative meeting area. The experiment has yielded cost savings ranging from 37 percent to 60 percent in real estate rent, construction, workspace services, furniture, IT equipment and services, and electric power.[24]

Cisco's estimates that its efforts to help workers be more mobile generate an extra hour of productivity per day per employee.[25] A 2008 study of approximately two thousand Cisco teleworkers in five global regions estimated that the company gains savings of $277 million in annual productivity, avoids more than 47,000 metric tons of greenhouse gas emissions, and saves employees more than $10 million in gasoline costs. The study also found that as many as 80 percent of employees felt career–life fit was better as a result, and more than 90 percent felt that working remotely was important to their overall satisfaction.[26]

In addition to redesigning the connected office, Cisco enables collaboration through a cutting-edge collection of tools that, not surprisingly, leverage its leadership role in the technology space to catalyze mass participation. Cisco has called it "The Human Network at Work." The tools include Ciscopedia (its own version of Wikipedia), YouTube-style video blogging on C-Vision, and Directory 3.0, Cisco's internal social network. CEO John Chambers is a high-profile contributor to C-Vision and prefers the format over text communication as a way to work around his dyslexia. At one point, Chambers was only the second-most-popular contributor, just behind a collaboration blog, and he narrowly edged out a director-level blogger several levels down from him in the hierarchy.[27] Beyond changing a formerly top-down culture and providing more avenues for employees to engage, Cisco estimates that these efforts have generated an almost $700 million business impact, a significant amount even for a large company.[28]

The collaborative, connected workplace also increases transparency, an ongoing emphasis in Cisco's effort to broaden avenues for participation. "If you don't drive transparency, you create blockages for the knowledge flow in the business, and then collaboration does not work," says Pond. "Collaboration fundamentally can't work without transparency."[29] He and other leaders have been active in video blogging, among other communication methods, so that they can deliver news—good and bad—candidly and directly.

Cisco's investments in virtual work and collaboration have also multiplied career options, showing the connections between the three lattice ways. Operations manager Carina Reyes says, "As a working mother of three children . . . I have the flexibility to choose the schedule that best fits my work and my home. Juggling early-morning Europe calls, midday doctor's appointments, and evening Asia meetings, I move with ease from one place to another. My family and I feel fortunate that I work for one of the best companies today that enables true work-life navigation."[30]

The company emphasizes that managers and employees should work together to develop solutions that are mutually beneficial.

Although it has not yet formally implemented career customization, Cisco policy encourages managers and employees to tailor how and when work happens around individual and business needs, demonstrating how a focus on enhancing the effectiveness of virtual work simultaneously expands opportunities to customize careers. "Giving people more options for when and where they work is one important way we expand the diversity of our workforce," says Marilyn Nagel, chief diversity officer.[31]

Cisco also applies the idea of customization to improve how college hires and interns start their careers. Called Cisco Choice, the program lets graduates pick their managers, and most are matched with one of their top three choices. The added options raise the engagement and retention of job-hopping Gen Yers. Following the program launch, 98 percent of these young people were still with the firm after two years.[32]

The company offers a high-growth environment with lots of opportunity. A key to navigating a career there is to take ownership. "We really do believe in empowering people to dream," explains Monaghan. "So many things are possible here. But with that empowerment comes a responsibility: employees need to know how to take care of themselves as well as the company."[33]

Adding It Up

Cisco's move away from a command-and-control style and toward less hierarchical means of participation provides insight into how lattice organizations evolve over the years. While the company looks forward to pushing the envelope further still, its path to date offers rich lessons. The initial focus was to expand cross-functional collaboration and increase productivity, embedding what we call lattice ways to work and participate into the business. But to achieve the full breadth of benefits, the efforts naturally moved into the related area of careers. And in each of these arenas, customization has grown.

Parts of Cisco's journey to becoming a lattice organization are at different stages of development, but in totality they show how each effort reinforces the others while propelling the company forward. The collaborative structure of councils and boards naturally evolved to address how leaders are developed and their careers are built. Lattice ways to participate collaboratively depended on new and more transparent ways of working that are more virtual and less bound by physical location or time constraints than the old ways. The virtual workplace, in turn, expanded options for customizing career–life fit.

All this work has paid off handsomely. As a mark of its achievements and importance to the economy, in mid-2009 Cisco was placed on the list of leading companies that constitute the Dow Jones Industrial Average. "Cisco makes the paving bricks for the information superhighway and it's affecting the culture in kind of the same way that automobiles affected the culture in the 20th century," says John A. Prestbo, editor and executive director of Dow Jones Indexes. "We thought it was a fitting replacement for General Motors."[34] Cisco's twenty-first-century lattice practices illuminate the path ahead for us all.

DELOITTE: ENABLING THE LATTICE ORGANIZATION

Deloitte, a nearly $11 billion professional services firm with forty-three thousand partners, principals, and employees in the United States and India, was at an inflection point in 2005.[35] It had doubled in size since 1996, making it difficult to sustain its hallmark collegial culture and shared values. It was also seeing a tectonic shift in its workforce and understood that its talent practices would need a similar jolt for the business to thrive. "In the professional services business, we have two assets—our clients and our people—and they are inextricably linked," says Deloitte LLP CEO

Barry Salzberg. "The caliber of our talent is fundamental to the success of our business."[36]

In 2005, women made up almost half of the organization's workforce, as well as 55 percent of accounting students nationally, a key talent pool for entry-level accounting positions.[37] Two-fifths of new hires in the United States and one-third of all personnel were minorities, and the trend was rising. More than five thousand personnel were now based in India, and many served global companies in a variety of locations, so virtual, collaborative teaming was frequent.

In addition, the generational differences in attitudes, aspirations, and family structures of Generations X and Y, which constituted 65 percent of the Deloitte workforce, challenged traditional models. Between 1992 and 2005, for instance, the percentage of men who wanted to become a partner or principal decreased by one-third, and for women the decline was 25 percent.[38] Growth experiences, however, were still a top priority: exit interviews showed that career opportunities were the most frequent reason cited in voluntary departures.[39] There were opportunities for what Bill Freda, managing partner, clients and markets, Deloitte LLP, refers to as "moments that matter," which he defines as "those instants in time that etch in the mind and shape the interest and willingness (or not) of each individual to engage."[40]

But the organization hadn't been sitting still. It was the first among its competitors to launch a women's initiative, with *BusinessWeek* noting that "few women's networks can boast of a track record like that of Deloitte."[41] It instituted a parallel diversity initiative to improve the representation of minority professionals at every level.[42] Deloitte had also designed and implemented a wide array of flexibility programs—sixty-nine, by one count—and it had made a significant commitment to building managers' coaching skills to improve on-the-job learning and development, part of what *Training + Development* magazine called a "living, breathing people strategy."[43]

Although each of its programs delivered some benefits, in aggregate the collective response wasn't hitting the mark. Deloitte offered numerous flexibility programs, for example, but lack of flexibility remained a top reason women as well as men left, according to exit interview data.[44]

Deloitte had to push talent innovation to a new level. Doing more of the same simply wouldn't be enough. And as it ventured further down its path, it found itself transforming, step by step, into a lattice organization.

Tailoring a Career Fit

Fast-forward to 2007, when Deloitte, after successfully piloting the mass career customization approach, began to implement the framework throughout its organization. As we explored in chapter 3, the MCC tool provides a structured approach for identifying career–life options, making choices, and understanding trade-offs over time so that value is created for individuals and for the business.

Deloitte began its first full wave of implementation with seventy-five hundred partners, principals, and employees across five businesses, followed by a rollout to another twenty-eight thousand people in 2008 and 2009. Its goal was to make operational a customized model that provided every individual with options for a sustainable career–life fit. Deloitte's implementation of the MCC tool has been hailed as a best-practice model. As Laura Fitzpatrick of *Time* notes, "Deloitte's Mass Career Customization program began as a way to keep talented women in the workforce, but it has quickly become clear that women are not the only ones seeking flexibility. [It responds] to millennials demanding better work-life balance, young parents needing time to share child-care duties, and boomers looking to ease gradually toward retirement."[45] One year after implementing the MCC framework and process, Deloitte had generated strong results from the initial rollouts (see figure 6-1).

FIGURE 6-1

Deloitte career–life fit satisfaction and quality of conversation improvement results

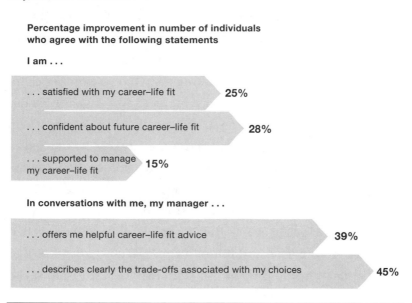

Percentage improvement in number of individuals who agree with the following statements

I am . . .

. . . satisfied with my career–life fit   25%

. . . confident about future career–life fit   28%

. . . supported to manage my career–life fit   15%

In conversations with me, my manager . . .

. . . offers me helpful career–life fit advice   39%

. . . describes clearly the trade-offs associated with my choices   45%

Option value particularly resonated with its people: satisfaction with career–life fit improved 25 percent, and confidence in future career–life fit improved 28 percent.[46] The organization also enjoyed large gains in the quality of career conversations. Overall, 88 percent of survey respondents had at least one career–life conversation with their managers or assigned counselors in the first post-MCC implementation year, and these respondents said that the quality of conversations was better by a ratio of 4 to 1. The improvement was particularly encouraging because the quality of conversations, considered a key factor in engagement, was previously known to be uneven. The MCC tool had upped the game of managers and counselors across the board.

MCC also directly boosted retention. High-performer retention improved twice as much in the areas that implemented the MCC tool compared with those that had not.[47] "MCC results drop right to our bottom line," says Joe Echevarria, managing partner, operations, Deloitte LLP. "Client satisfaction, revenue, retention, productivity—all are impacted by how our people are able to fit life into work and work into life."[48]

Experiences in the field show how the MCC process works in practice. Jia Li Moore, now a senior manager at Deloitte Consulting LLP, decided to dial up, initiating a stretch role on her client project. She excelled and earned a promotion. "We all drive our own careers, so if you're going to drive really fast one year, it's up to you to find those opportunities," she says. Mike Ranken, a manager in enterprise risk services, Deloitte & Touche LLP, chose the common profile. He and his manager used the MCC profile to fully explore his interest in global assignments. And Mike Jacobson, a senior associate in Deloitte Financial Advisory Services LLP, dialed down to pursue an MBA part-time. Jacobson believes that solid preparation and early buy in from his managers were key to developing a career–life fit that works for him.[49]

These stories, and the organization's significant results, testify to two fundamental benefits of the MCC framework. The first is option value—the comfort individuals experience when they know there is a way to customize their careers as priorities evolve over time, even if they don't make adjustments at any given moment. Second, the MCC process offers participation value—the trust and engagement that result from transparent conversations about the benefits and trade-offs of career–life options.

The first wave of rollouts paved the way for subsequent waves and led Deloitte to several important conclusions. An initial concern that didn't materialize was that the MCC framework would open the floodgates for those who wanted to dial down and the organization would not be able to staff its client commitments. But no more than 10 percent of individuals have elected to dial up or down at any point in time.[50]

Some people in Deloitte challenged this outcome, asking why the organization should implement the MCC tool when only 10 percent of individuals opted to dial up or down. "Although the vast majority of people chose not to dial in any particular direction right now, they are watching the 10 percent who do to see how the options we offer work," explains James Jaeger, managing partner, talent, Deloitte LLP. "Choices will change, and a different 10 percent will cycle through. Over time, closer to 90 percent will have turned a dial at some point in time."[51] Indeed, Deloitte reports that about 40 percent of participants have explored the dial-up and dial-down options and comments that whether or not they exercise a change right now, there is high value in the greater planning for future options, transparent information exchanges, and more in-depth career conversations.[52]

Another lesson was that the value of looking at things as an integrated whole was well worth the extra effort. Because Deloitte embedded the MCC approach into existing talent management processes such as goal setting, performance management, talent development, and deployment, MCC became a lattice tool, and not a one-off program that didn't connect to a larger effort.

Deloitte continues to measure and monitor the impact of the MCC tool and continuously improve it. Now, more than thirty-five thousand partners, principals, and employees participate in MCC, and the organization plans to have the framework and process in place to cover its entire workforce by June 2010.

But just as the full impact of its MCC approach was being felt, Deloitte discovered additional applications of customization.

Raising the Game in Talent Development

Picking up on the business case for customized options, Deloitte began weaving customization into its talent development strategy. "There is no longer a single development path," says Bill Pelster, chief learning officer, Deloitte LLP. "Not only are there more options for destinations in a lattice, but there are also multiple ways to journey toward any given destination."[53]

To customize learning, more than 2.4 million hours of instruction are being retooled so that people can tailor their learning. And curricula are being redesigned. "Individuals are unique," says Pelster, "so we are creating a learning experience that is personalized."[54] Individuals can opt out of courses in which they demonstrate command of the subject matter, or they can take courses geared to their individual knowledge gaps—making learning more engaging and productive. Learning and growth options also integrate with the MCC framework.

Deloitte has announced a $300 million investment in Deloitte University, a state-of-the-art campus for learning and leadership development scheduled to open in 2011. Technology-fluent Gen Yers were one of the most vocal constituencies in favor of Deloitte U. "As our work has become more virtual, the need for a shared experience to build community, connection, and culture has grown, too," says Barry Salzberg. "Deloitte University is a very tangible expression of our commitment to our people and their development."[55]

Deloitte's design for Deloitte University extends well beyond the physical campus. The facility will be networked with every major office via videoconference teleclassrooms. It will also be connected to online classrooms for anywhere, anytime learning that fits in with the virtual style of lattice ways to work. The learning design includes wiki-based electronic communities so that collaborative and transparent lattice ways to participate can be extended beyond the classroom.

Anytime, Anywhere Work and Participation

At the same time that it was scaling its MCC approach, Deloitte launched the Workplace of the Future initiative to further expand its fifteen-year-old program of office space hoteling and remote work capabilities. Many professionals work at their clients' locations rather than in Deloitte offices, so mobile computing was already a way of life for many people.

The Workplace of the Future program created more ways for individuals to customize how they work. For example, a new voice mail system enables a work phone to forward to a cell phone or other number, and voice mails now arrive in e-mail inboxes. High-end videoconference telesuites were built to reduce travel and lend an interactive and in-person feeling to meetings.

These and other solutions have resulted in a 30 percent reduction in square footage per person and a 30 percent savings in energy costs—for an overall savings of more than $100 million per year after more than two years of implementation.[56] And the Workplace of the Future has increased the MCC framework's Location and Schedule options for when and where work happens, expanding options for customizing careers.

Meanwhile, a parallel and connected change was going on in the ways Deloitte's people participate in the organization. As part of its broader efforts to innovate, in 2006 the organization launched Innovation Quest, an annual contest open to all. Individuals or teams submit ideas or vote on others' ideas for new client service offerings and internal process improvements. Since its inception, eighteen hundred people have submitted more than twelve hundred ideas, of which forty-four winners have been selected.[57] "In more traditional structures, just a few departments were charged with innovation," says John Levis, chief strategy officer, Deloitte LLP. "At Deloitte, we are making innovation a part of our organizational DNA so everyone can contribute. If we can tap in to the full diversity of our talent's experiences and perspectives, we'll deliver more value to clients and a more stimulating work environment to our people."[58]

Building on this innovation, in 2008 Deloitte launched D Street, the cornerstone of its efforts to increase community and connection across the enterprise. "We want Deloitte to be a place where everyone feels welcome, valued, and connected," explains Sharon Allen, chairman of the board, Deloitte LLP. "D Street makes it possible to do that across the boundaries of time and distance. It also helps promote our efforts to be even more inclusive of the diverse backgrounds and experiences our people bring to the table."[59]

Deloitte's design envisioned an online platform to build the networks that connect people, enhance careers, and enable the right teams to form across the organization. The social networking site acts as a virtual watercooler, with individuals tailoring their own pages with personal and professional information. From there, communities emerge. For example, the owners of Harley-Davidson motorcycles found each other and started a community page based on their shared interest, which dovetailed with the network of professionals who serve this client.

Deloitte encouraged personnel to use D Street to build their personal brands and to "think of D Street as your personal storefront—the place where you can display your wares and tell the rest of the organization what you have to offer."[60] Public relations, for example, found on D Street an employee for *BusinessWeek* to photograph: Cedric Nabe, an Olympian in training. He gained valuable exposure in the process. Blogs are another way D Street builds brands and connects people. Deloitte Tax LLP CEO Chet Wood blogs on D Street about everything from marathons to his trip to India. He says he's "gaining a greater perspective on what's on the minds of our people."[61] Wood is not alone. More than two thousand blogs are active on D Street, many written by partners, principals, and directors, and this in turn makes leadership more accessible and transparent.

Thirteen months after full deployment of the site, Deloitte reports that about 90 percent of partners, principals, and employees have visited it at least once, and almost half have personalized their profiles, attached pictures, or posted a blog. Participants have created more than eleven thousand affiliations to business resource groups and programs such as communities of practice—for example, the "Go Green" initiative. D Street now averages almost six hundred visitors per day and houses twenty-five thousand personalized profiles and seven thousand resumes.[62] In 2008,

ComputerWorld highlighted D Street to showcase Deloitte's best practices in the "early adoption of internal social networking."[63] Yet another aspect of the lattice has taken shape.

Concerted Efforts

As Deloitte reviewed its progress, it saw that hierarchical and siloed ways of building careers, working, and participating were rapidly fading. To power the organization's talent-driven business strategy, customization became an increasingly important part of every talent-related initiative. In the process, Deloitte was finally cracking the code on its flexibility challenges, helping it attract and retain a wider range of people. It was seeing itself as a career enhancer that provided employees, partners and principals multiple options to grow and develop. And once it began to overlay existing initiatives on the lattice model, it became plain that these efforts were combining organically in response to the shift from ladder to lattice. No single change was transforming the culture; all were working in concert.

Deloitte's results demonstrate the value of lattice-style investments as well as the mind-set shift they require. From 2006 to 2008, revenues grew 25 percent and client satisfaction rose, fueled in part by gains on the people front. The rates of both voluntary turnover and top-performer attrition steadily declined.[64] Engagement and average tenure also improved over the same period, as did the acceptance rates of job offers extended to campus as well as experienced hires.[65] And Deloitte reached a milestone in the organization's history by exceeding the one thousand mark for women partners, principals, and directors—the highest number of any firm in the profession.

Among other distinctions, Deloitte earned the top spot on *BusinessWeek*'s Best Places to Launch a Career list and on its Best Places to Intern in 2009, moved up thirty-five spots on the 2009 *Fortune* 100 Best Companies to Work For list, and ranked on both the *DiversityInc* and the *Working Mother* lists of the best companies to work for.[66] It was also inducted into *Training* magazine's Hall of Fame—an honor bestowed on only six other companies.[67] In 2009, the *Shriver Report* stated that Deloitte "provides an excellent example of an employer that has taken an aggressive leadership position in protean career approaches."[68] And to top it off, it received the 2010 Catalyst Award, in large part because of its innovative lattice thinking and the results it engenders.[69] In Deloitte's case, its bold embrace of the lattice is helping it capture market share, serve clients better, and craft a more engaging talent experience.

A TRANSFORMATION AT THOMSON REUTERS FINANCE

By the turn of the twenty-first century, the Thomson Reuters legacy business model was reaching its limits. The $13 billion leader in information services for professionals had enjoyed a proud history dating to 1934, when Roy Thomson bought his first newspaper, *The Timmins Press,* in Ontario, Canada.[70] From that humble start, the company grew into a media giant focused on electronic information services, ultimately divesting itself of its heritage newspaper business. But it remained a portfolio of independent companies.

In the Thomson Financial division, this structure was problematic. "We were operating as a portfolio of little companies, and as a result, we were not achieving the benefits of our scale to effectively challenge more unified competitors," says Sharon Rowlands, then-CEO of Thomson Financial.[71] In response, Thomson Financial launched a major transformation to consolidate forty-two smaller companies and form larger operating units, bringing together centralized sales, service, technology, finance, and content groups.

One day in 2006, David Turner, executive vice president and current CFO of Thomson Reuters Markets, was sitting in his office in downtown Manhattan. He had just finished a call with Bob Daleo, CFO of the parent company, and Daleo had asked Turner to take a new job leading a transformational effort, called Finance-Plus, that Daleo had designed for the finance organization. Turner reflected on the scale of the change that needed to be made. Each of the portfolio companies had a complete finance group: everything from forecasting and planning to accounts receivable and accounts payable sat under a CFO. Under Daleo's new strategy, many finance roles at the divisional level would be eliminated, and the accounting resources of the businesses would be combined under two division presidents.[72]

The structure would need to change from vertical silos toward the more horizontal lattice orientation. Not only would the move create economies of scale to address mounting cost pressures, but also it would help meet the requirements of increased levels of regulation and offer greater career–life and development options to attract and retain top finance talent. Turner embraced the challenge.

From Silos to Service Bureaus

To dismantle silos, specialized service bureaus brought together common accounting functions, and much smaller finance teams remained in the businesses. Freed of routine operations, the divisional role was to provide specialized analytics and business advice.

With both Thomson and Reuters predecessor companies having a significant presence in Bangalore, India, it was surprising that the finance division did not operate there.[73] So for routine finance functions, India became the operations center, and nearly one in five finance professionals works there today. For activities that required greater interaction with the business, regional bureaus were set up in North America, Asia, and Europe.

During the transition, the company migrated to a common set of financial systems. Joint planning, forecasting, transaction, and reporting systems were adopted. "Moving to the new systems was mandatory, not optional," says Turner. "Without common systems, you can't build common processes or proper service bureaus."[74] Anna Patruno, global head of financial business operations for the division, adds, "Even though we serve diverse markets with different products, our business models are very similar. The commonality of our processes is far greater than our differences."[75]

The improvements have given the organization new levels of transparency and flexibility. A universal forecasting tool offers all levels access to the same data in real time, and a rolling eighteen-month forecast now adds more visibility into what the future may have in store. Low-value activities like data collating and collecting are on the decline. On the rise is value-added analysis that can drive better business decisions.

Virtual Teams, Tangible Results

Global operations require lattice ways of working. Teams rather than individuals now provide service to the businesses, and that necessitates sharing knowledge transparently (information must be shared on common platforms that everyone can access) so that when one team member is offline, another can seamlessly cover for him or her.

And teams now span the globe. "Instead of getting information from the guy sitting next to you in Boston, you now teleconference with the team in Bangalore," says Patruno.[76] "It doesn't always run smoothly: you have to adjust your time-frame thinking and be willing to do meetings early in the morning or late at night to manage other calendars and other time zones. Not everyone was really interested in that, although most people accepted the challenge."

The technology infrastructure has had to be upgraded as well. Telepresence rooms are in all major offices, and desktop-based videoconferences are a regular part of the way work is done. And the workplace itself is being redesigned for mobility. The London office, for instance, has a completely open floor plan. A significant portion of the office has temporary rather than permanent desks. It is all part of the company's Smart Working plan. As Ivan Newman, a senior project manager in property management, explains, "The end result is that we could make much better use of the office space within the building, and at the same time, allow employees far greater flexibility in terms of their work-life balance."[77]

Global, 24/7 operations also demand flexibility in work schedules. Meetings are often scheduled for the business day in Bangalore, so it is the staff located in North America or Europe who have the odd hours. People need a high degree of formal and informal flexibility to get their work done, and options like compressed workweeks and telecommuting are popular. Employee survey results show the benefit: a clear majority (80 percent) rate the company's flexibility efforts favorably, five points higher than the average at other high-performing firms.[78]

The new lattice ways of working also give the organization flexibility. In the past, seldom did more than a few select people see the total picture of any particular business. Now entire teams understand how things work, creating modularity in jobs. Projects can be staffed in multiple ways based on the needs of the moment.

Initially, all these new ways of working were foreign to many managers accustomed to having the people reporting to them sitting together in the same office, in the line of sight. Says Turner, "At first it didn't make sense to people that managers could lead people in other locations or that we could build a team culture across geographies. Over time, employees realized if you utilize technologies and different ways of communicating, people can be just as effective remotely as they can sitting next door to you."[79]

Adds Patruno, "Technology has advanced so much that we're much more able to manage remotely. But it does take a mind shift, because managers really have to understand that they don't have to be the clock-checker. They just need to learn to make an extra investment in setting clear goals and time frames and giving clear guidance and direction. Then the team can deliver."[80]

It took only about six months for people in the divisions to see that they could get even better results. When services were shared, costs were lower and more resources could be brought to bear during crunch times. Finance leaders actively modeled the new way of doing business, and "this really helped people to change their ways of working in a relatively short time," explains Matthew Burkley, CFO of the sales and trading division.[81]

Up or Over

In the past, the ultimate position in Turner's organization was CFO, and many strived to get there as quickly as possible. "Your job was to get more and more general with each job promotion," says Burkley. But "in the new organization, with each new job, you want to build up a collection of deep capabilities so that when you migrate into a generalist role, you're much better prepared. You build a series of specific competencies that then allow you to be a strong generalist."

These days, career planning is designed around a defined sequence of experiences. To move beyond the initial layer of management, professionals need a mix of positions in finance operations, the corporate finance organization, a finance division, and a business unit. "Each of these experiences builds the total perspective of finance," says Turner.[82] "Now someone can go from a business unit to a new geography to a corporate center to a division center, which provides a lot more variety, a lot more challenge, and a lot more learning." Important jobs also exist in running service centers or managing key initiatives that cut across the organization. And there's now an elaborate system of recognition and rewards—including a high-profile awards ceremony and significant recognition for winners—that makes it prestigious to deliver results rather than prestigious only to be promoted.[83]

The result? People can develop along many routes and can see clearly how to get valuable career-enhancing experiences. "Experience used to be seen very much vertically, moving from junior to senior roles," Turner says. "Nowadays experiences from moving across the organization are what make people really valuable to us."[84]

Transparent Voices

As the Thomson Reuters finance division evolved, it found it needed a better means to communicate and engage with its people. No longer could employees expect to get most of the information they needed from their local manager. In the emerging modes of participation, local managers often needed information just as much as their employees did. And feedback from employee surveys showed that one-way, top-down communication was not working. Employees felt their voices and concerns were not being heard. A new model was needed.

So the finance organization replaced dry e-mails and webcasts with town hall meetings, interactive global videoconferences, and even a radio show with audience participation. Listeners call or e-mail with questions, and the entire finance leadership responds, candidly laying out issues as well as opportunities. "Today we provide a lot more authentic discussion," says Turner. "Being transparent builds trust, which really makes the division into a community rather than a bunch of silos."

The finance division has also given a role traditionally reserved for management—identifying improvement priorities—to employees. It launched a "pain points" portal, where employees voice their view of current challenges for everyone to see. But the portal is more than a suggestion box: the pain points are categorized, triaged, and then managed based on the volume of complaints. Most of the concerns are handed off to appointed pain-point owners, who bring together teams of relevant experts from across the company to solve the issues. They identify the severity of the problem and how to address it; they post their plan and, later, the progress made.

Early on, for example, most pain points revolved around the financial close. Within three months of working to implement employee suggestions, a team had reduced a tangle of complex issues so that it became "incredibly smooth and simplified," says Patruno.[85] "By having employees articulate the pain point and then actually fix it, we increase employee engagement, because people can see their ideas generating results." The proof: an improvement of 11 percentage points in employee engagement during the first year after the strategy was implemented.[86]

Collaboration is now a key value of the finance organization and an important performance expectation. A lot of training went into helping employees work across the organization in remote, often international, teams, and new metrics for performance were adopted that emphasize teamwork and results across boundaries. Thomson Reuters calls it "working the network." Employee surveys substantiate the beneficial results. In one year, the survey metric for collaboration and global mind-set increased 15 percent, to 88 percent of employees rating the organization favorably on this attribute.[87]

"Before, to get results you just worked within your existing little sandbox," says Patruno. "In the new structure, you have to work the network, and you have to rely on people in different places. You have to get them aligned and motivated to make things happen. And so it's a very different style of working through influence and relationships. Your point of affiliation with the company has gone from your direct manager to the broader finance organization."[88]

Closing the Gap

The FinancePlus transition to service bureaus has thus far yielded approximately $50 million in annual savings.[89] It also helps leaders make better decisions and delivers improved forecasting and planning. Regulatory compliance functions are stronger now, too, and employee engagement is up.

When David Turner took on the challenge of reinventing the finance division, he didn't set out specifically to create a lattice organization. But as he steered it away from a traditional vertical hierarchy to a more matrixed and horizontal structure, the lattice began to take shape. The workforce became globally integrated, and work itself became virtual and team oriented. Career paths, in response, naturally focused more on the growth of expertise and lateral movements than they had previously.

It all adds up to new and varied options for fitting career and life together. Turner sums it up this way:

> For a business to keep the best talent and keep them motivated, there have to be sustainable ways of working. In days gone by, a key problem was that people could ask for flexibility, but they felt like they were putting an end to their career if they did. The younger generations are both more determined and confident in their ability to have more than just work. And I find myself intermingling my work life and my nonwork life almost seamlessly. And that seamless inter-mingling of the two basically makes both of them better and neither of them overwhelming.[90]

The change also demanded a focus on transparency and collaboration, which in turn meant giving everyone a voice and a chance to contribute. Performance expectations and recognition evolved to support the new ways of thinking and acting. Citing constant reinforcement from the top, Turner confirms that, indeed, the finance division has transitioned to a lattice view and is reaping the benefits that this orientation brings.[91]

Cisco, Deloitte, and Thomson Reuters are three strong and yet varied examples of the lattice organization in practice. Their journeys, although not complete, are quite far along, and each illustrates lattice ways of crafting individualized and yet inclusive experiences, as well as the value they can produce. In chapter 7, we shift our focus to the implications of lattice living for those who make up the heart of the organization: individuals.

7 ► THE INDIVIDUAL'S GUIDE TO THE SHIFTING LANDSCAPE

Chance favors the prepared mind.

—*Louis Pasteur*

WHILE OPPORTUNITY MAY FAVOR those who are prepared to succeed, the corporate lattice is changing the rules about how people succeed in the first place. The promise of the corporate lattice is that it gives us all more ways to chart our own paths. The price it exacts, however, is that each of us must be more aware of our options and more intentional about our choices.

"Employees own their own careers," says Robyn Denholm, CFO at Juniper Networks. "Career ownership is 99 percent their job and 1 percent the organization's job."[1] It is in your best interest to steer your own career journey rather than ride along as a passenger. Says Pattie Sellers, *Fortune* magazine's editor at large, "Think of the lattice as a jungle gym. The best opportunities to broaden your

FIGURE 7-1

Comparison of ladder and lattice thinking for the individual

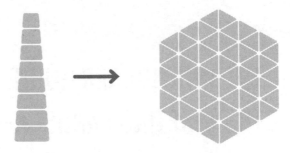

- Coworkers with similar backgrounds, experiences, and models of success
- Limited options for when, where, and how work gets done
- Destination jobs
- Separation of work and life
- Emphasis on vertical progression

- Coworkers with diverse backgrounds, experiences, and models of success
- Many options for when, where, and how work gets done
- Varied possible roles
- Work fits into life and life fits into work
- Emphasis on continued growth and development

experience may be lateral or even down. Look every which way and swing to opportunities."[2]

The differences between the ladder and the lattice with respect to the individual are shown in figure 7-1. The good news: you have choices that for too long have been static—from the way your work is done to the intensity of your contributions to the trajectory of your career. The bad news: you need to choose, and not only once or twice at particular inflection points but repeatedly as you move through the stages of your life and as the ever-changing marketplace evolves.

Navigating the corporate lattice is less about aiming for a single lifetime career destination and more about expanding your portfolio of capabilities and experiences so that you continually have options that are valuable to both you and your employer. Success requires a perspective of mutual benefit and active choice. In this last chapter, we offer several strategies to help you navigate your lattice journey.

- **Think option value:** No one knows exactly what life has in store, so the greater the number of possible future choices, the greater their value to you. To orient your career for greater option value, you need to seek out learning experiences, develop transferable skills, and contribute broadly throughout organizational networks.

- **Mark to market your individual assets:** Your capabilities are, in essence, intangible assets for you and your company. But assets of many kinds grow obsolete at much faster rates now than in the past, and so, too, can your relevance fade. Periodically inventory your brand's value just as businesses do. Compare your skills and experiences with those of colleagues in your field, and look further down the road to understand what will be valued in the future.

- **Optimize career–life fit:** Much as an investor faces competing risk and reward objectives, you confront competing choices about how to develop your career in tandem with your life. Only through collaboration with your employer can you together understand trade-offs, devise creative solutions, and craft an optimal fit amid divergent goals.

THINK OPTION VALUE

In the field of scenario planning, strategists are skilled in helping companies imagine and plan for multiple plausible futures. Adaptive strategies that play well across many scenarios allow for additional maneuvering and multiply the choices that create option value in a dynamic environment. Similarly, you enjoy greater *career* option value when you proactively anticipate possibilities and expand the number of future choices. By investing in transferable skills, for example, you can hedge against unforeseen market shifts and, on the upside, gain options for growth and development and for fitting life and work together.

It's 10 o'clock. Do you know what your options are?

You most likely have a grasp of your portfolio of skills and capabilities as well as your probable career path if the talent market and your life circumstances remain relatively constant. But planning for a dynamic and complex future is much more difficult. If you are like many people, asking "what if" is a bit like saving for a rainy day—hard to do when the sun is blazing.

What if the company reorganizes—what else could you do to contribute, and who would want you on his or her team? What if your life changes course and you transition from single to married or no kids to kids, from few family responsibilities to elder care demands? What if you get a once-in-a-lifetime chance to pursue a lifelong passion in, say, volunteer work, sports, the arts, or travel? Or what if your area of specialty becomes obsolete seemingly overnight, as some people in the financial sector experienced during the abrupt economic downturn that started in 2007?

These are the kinds of questions that Thomson Reuters's Matthew Burkley has intuitively asked in his own career journey. He started as an analyst for a professional services firm because, as he puts it, "the role offered a high option value."[3] The wide exposure it provided to various industries and companies opened up many career possibilities down the road. Then he stepped away from full-time work to attend Harvard Business School—another option-creating move that built transferable skills for a range of career choices.

After graduation, swept up in the spirit of the mid-1990s, Burkley cofounded an Internet company. His career was fully dialed up—to use an MCC term—as he expanded the venture over nearly five years and then sold his majority ownership position. For the next few years, he dialed down his career and did some writing and independent consulting. From there he leveraged his portfolio of transferable skills in the corporate world, joining Thomson Corporation as senior vice president of business operations in the financial division—a new role that Burkley describes as "having no job description but to make my boss's problems, my problems."

He gained valuable skills in navigating a large, complex firm, and he demonstrated what he was made of. He was subsequently tapped to take over a newly created role as head of strategy for the financial division and then went on to manage a business within the same division.

When Thomson and Reuters merged, Burkley moved into another strategy role to help with the merger and subsequent integration. Recently, wanting to get closer to the operations side, he accepted a chief financial officer position for the sales and trading division—a lateral move organizationally, but one that provides a breadth of opportunity. He is learning a new part of the business in trading and is living in a new location in London.

When plotted over time, Burkley's journey looks like a sine wave (see figure 7-2). Rather than focus exclusively on the next logical, linear rung, he has chosen to design his career for optimum option value. He is prepared for whatever future opportunity presents itself. "I could never have planned out the roles that I've had," he says, "and although I have ideas of what might come next, I don't want to predict nor constrain myself by any [single] possibility."

In a similar fashion, you too should look ahead—and left and right—at potential roles that are of interest to you, where your skills are transferable and likely to remain relevant in the future. A lateral move or a special project may be just the way to round out your capabilities and better position you for whatever comes next.

It's important to find a balance between gaining expertise and seeking breadth to keep future options open. "You want to be very flexible in your career and put yourself in nontraditional circumstances and job assignments, but at the same time hold on to a depth of expertise that will carry you throughout your career," says General Mills chief learning officer Kevin Wilde.[4]

FIGURE 7-2

Mathew Burkley's lattice career jouney

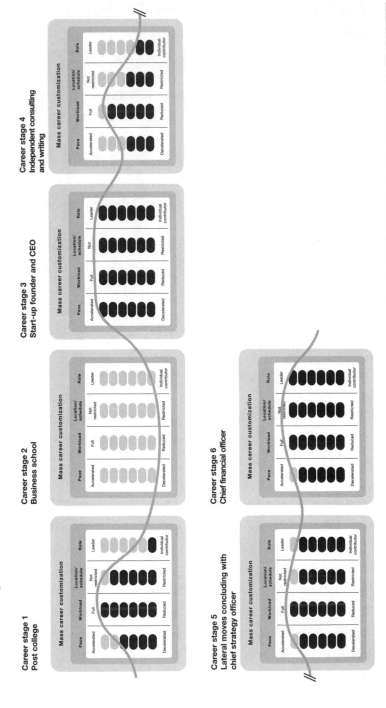

In a traditional ladder approach, you invest in preparing for each vertical step. Along the lattice, however, you invest in things that give you strategic flexibility—even if they don't net an immediate payoff. The goal of your investment strategy is to develop your marketability, something that in turn offers you more choices in the future.

Employers, too, are looking for individuals who have option value. Companies need people who can take on a variety of fluid assignments. "Roles are simply more fungible than traditionally," says Robyn Denholm. "Relevance of skills, experiences, and competencies is what we look for most. We are looking at potential hires for what the individual can contribute. They each play a role in the organization, but the bounds of the roles are more opaque."[5]

Silicon Valley veteran and user experience expert Harry Max has deliberately built a portfolio of skills through a series of lateral moves. "I wanted to be the best in my field, but at the same time, I knew I didn't want to stay in any one field forever," he explains.[6] Through a series of horizontal jumps into related fields, often at the same company, Max gained experience in many parts of the software business, from gathering and understanding customer needs to writing documentation to marketing, selling, and supporting the finished product.

He began his career writing online technical manuals and developing training for Santa Cruz Operation and then moved to Silicon Graphics, Inc. (SGI), in a technical communication role. From there he decided to transition into a technical marketing communication role at SGI, which moved him from the product to the marketing side of the business, where he was responsible for product packaging, sales training, and marketing communication. "I realized that user documentation, by definition, was a defect, because needing to document how to do something meant that the product wasn't obvious," says Max. This insight was instrumental in his moving to HaL Computer Systems, where, as a user experience strategist on the product marketing team, he was tasked with defining the total out-of-box experience for customers. His goal: to maximize the intuitiveness of features so that software required less training and documentation.

Although not linear, these steps had natural connections. Max leveraged the skills he developed while staying engaged and highly productive. As a postscript to Max's journey, he went on to cofound Virtual Vineyards, the online wine retailer now known as Wine.com. Here, he created the first secure online shopping cart, which soon became a feature of all e-commerce sites.[7] The achievement was more profound than any documentation Max could have created had he stayed in his original position.

Some people might argue that moving across business units or positions carries great risk, because you enter areas where you don't know the subject or the players and where you might not have an aptitude for the work. A vertical promotion can be seen as a safer path to career growth.

We disagree. Learning and development are vital to creating future options. Moves that lower your risk of becoming obsolete— sometimes through a "risky" stretch assignment laterally—may be safer in the long run than waiting for a vertical promotion to come along.

Anne Mulcahy, chairman of Xerox, notes that she came up through the sales organization and with each rung was given bigger budgets and assignments. Although she was "scaling the ladder" over time, she wasn't stretching, and that is one reason she was attracted to an entirely different area of the company— human resources—which she believed had the potential to be a powerful part of the organization. Mulcahy refers to her career pathway as a series of "lateral arabesques."[8] Her horizontal move to HR allowed her to make a more profound mark on the firm and proved to be a decision that eventually led her to become CEO and later chairman.

Option-Creating Strategies

- **Build a portfolio of career-enhancing skills and experiences.**
  Take risks that get you out of your comfort zone.

- **Develop transferable skills.** Lateral moves, special-project
  assignments, leadership development programs, and outside-
  of-work experience all can be helpful.

- **Be an agile learner.** Learning agility is the competency that
  most correlates with success in a wide range of management
  and leadership activities. Whether you grow in place, move laterally, or step up, don't let inertia seep in.

- **Choose companies wisely.** Seek out employers that offer a variety of options for developing talents and building careers.

Xerox views arabesques like Mulcahy's as a strategy to develop
high-potential employees. For example, the company practices
lean six sigma, a set of processes and an organizational discipline
that Mulcahy notes "has a lot to do with taking out waste through
taking out bureaucracy and hierarchy." Xerox trains people to be
"black belts," or lean six sigma experts, by taking them outside
their roles and providing them with a completely different experience. Xerox calls it "breadth-building."

The point is that lateral moves are key to future vertical ones.
Once considered nontraditional, horizontal leaps along the corporate lattice are fast becoming expected.

We've shown how nontraditional career moves can open up
new possibilities, but there's more you can do. Your choice of
employer can also increase your options dramatically. Favor firms
that offer multiple approaches to customizing your growth experiences and career–life fit, because they provide greater option value

than companies that don't. Companies that enable customized careers frequently have such features as lateral *and* vertical career pathways, job-rotation programs, global assignments, varied skill-development opportunities, and career–life options. They provide many ways to participate, so if you take the initiative to join in, you have more ways to learn and become known to others.

Transparent information about how companies customize careers has become widely available. For example, *BusinessWeek*'s Best Places to Launch a Career list includes information on developmental rotations, mentoring, and spending on training per employee. By choosing employers that offer a range of possibilities, you have a greater chance of capitalizing on an options orientation.

MARK TO MARKET YOUR INDIVIDUAL ASSETS

In addition to generating option value and becoming more nimble, you should also address the *source* of your value to others. You must mark to market your individual assets.

In accounting terms, marking assets to market is a method businesses use to properly recognize the current value of each asset on the balance sheet. You can use a similar "outside-in" perspective to value your own acquired skills, knowledge, and experiences as the market sees them. In that way, you can stay relevant for whatever future may unfold.

Work requires significantly higher skill levels than formerly: in the 1960s, 30 percent of jobs required postsecondary training, whereas now 85 percent of jobs do. Skills and knowledge are also growing obsolete far faster than in the past.[9] A 2009 survey revealed that more than 75 percent of workers across generations believe in the necessity of upgrading skills within the next five years to keep up with changes in the workplace.[10] To stay up-to-date, treat "what you know" as a work in progress that requires continuous improvement.

Individuals risk falling behind simply by failing to move forward. "One of the scariest things someone can tell me is that they've been doing the same thing the same way for five years," says John DiMare, partner at executive search firm Crown Advisors. "They can't see that everyone else has gotten better and more productive. They just didn't stay current."[11] Don't become complacent, even during long-term jobs. Gordon Gee, president of The Ohio State University, likens the skill-building process to a dance: "You need to keep your dance card full even when you don't want to switch partners."[12]

Your mark-to-market individual asset value is a function of the portfolio of capabilities that you have developed. In short, it is the value of your personal brand.

Legendary ad agency founder David Ogilvy once defined a brand as the intangible sum of a product's attributes: its name, packaging, and price; its history; its reputation; and how it is advertised.[13] Later, in a 1997 *Fast Company* article titled "The Brand Called You," management guru Tom Peters applied the notion of branding to workers. In the article, employees are encouraged to escape the confines of their job description and define what makes them different from their colleagues. Once you define what you offer (the features) and the value you create (the benefits), Peters advocates marketing and communicating "the brand called You" through all means possible.[14]

Your brand is an intangible asset that must be defined and customized, consistently communicated through your actions and results, and continually refined and invested in. Your brand represents a cross-section of who you are and what others perceive you to be. It is your calling card, shorthand for your reputation and your value proposition.

The strength of your individual portfolio of assets including your personal brand is a function of the following:

- How well you develop a breadth and depth of skills and experiences that the market finds valuable and distinctive

- How well you articulate the benefits of that mix

- How well you make known the value proposition of your personal brand to others

Organizations are filled with people of widely differing backgrounds, skills, and experiences. Your value proposition—what you offer in abilities, accomplishments, and the experience of others in working with you—are all factors in the brand promise that you communicate and that others communicate about you.

Regularly comparing your value proposition with those of colleagues and peers, both inside and outside the company, can help you determine your brand's strengths and weaknesses and identify any opportunities for improvement. It also ensures that you are growing in areas that benefit your organization and increase your future marketability. It helps you mark to market your personal brand.

At BT, as you saw in chapter 5, the role of hierarchy has been evolving, and, with it, the importance of personal brands has risen. The company focuses less on who reports to whom and more on the work that needs to be done and the skills needed to do it. "Today it is expertise and reputation in the organization that count more than the status of the position," says principal business partner Richard Dennison.[15]

Alan Miller, CEO of Universal Health Services, puts it this way: "Your work follows you. Don't think that when you work for a company, you're doing the company a favor. Have pride in your work. It's your record. You carry it with you."[16]

Getting honest feedback is critical to understanding how the market values your brand. Peters suggests constructing the equivalent of a software "user's group" and soliciting honest and constructive feedback on your performance, your growth, and your value.[17] You can then accurately fill in the gaps that might exist between what you can do now and what you are able to do in the future.

Being clear on the value you deliver and your development goals also enables the organization to partner with you in achieving your growth objectives. Managers constantly decide whom to invest in developing as tasks, projects, and even jobs open up. If your personal brand stands out as more compelling and persuasive than those of others, it will help managers connect you to career-enhancing opportunities that are a fit for you, greatly assisting you in customizing your career.

Personal branding isn't a spectator sport. It isn't enough simply to have a reputation. Like any product's brand, the value of your personal brand is determined by how many people know your brand and believe it delivers what it represents. You should communicate your brand clearly to those you know so that they can communicate it to the people *they* know. The many lattice ways of participating explored in chapter 5 open up a host of brand-building opportunities.

In a networked environment, as many as 85 percent of positions are never advertised, according to Randall Hansen, associate professor of marketing at Stetson University.[18] Relationships, word of mouth, and targeted job postings are essential to being matched with challenging assignments that allow you to stretch. Growing and maintaining a strong brand identity are particularly important for one overarching reason: the stronger your brand, the more top-of-mind it is to your network, which can screen and refer opportunities to you. Those future possibilities in turn increase your option value.

Of course, the transparent information available today makes it easier to be long remembered for things you'd rather not be known for. Actor Tom Cruise is widely viewed as having damaged his reputation for several years after his 2005 couch-jumping declaration of love for Katie Holmes on *Oprah*. Similar challenges on a smaller scale occur when less-than-flattering information becomes part of the permanent record about you available online—from an embarrassing photo to disappointing project results. The information that a public Internet search reveals about you can shape your reputation, too, and yet only 3 percent of Internet users regularly monitor online information about themselves.[19]

Transparency also has made individual brands easier to see through. Information technology, for example, has made it quicker and easier to thoroughly fact-check resumes. According to a CareerBuilder.com survey, nearly half of hiring managers report they have found lies on resumes.[20] One technique employers use is to compare current resume submissions with prior ones stored electronically and then flag discrepancies. Recruiters at attorney search consultants Major, Lindsey & Africa, for example, are trained to spot inconsistencies, have access to twenty-five years of resume submissions to the firm, and regularly run Internet searches on applicants.[21]

Developing and promoting your personal brand are high priorities in the lattice world, because it is less likely that those directly within your present work group or department alone will determine your continued growth. In chapter 5, for example, we describe how Goldman Sachs colleagues across geographic locations, business lines, and functional groups all contribute feedback.

Lattice ways of working, too, raise the stakes of personal brands, because teams are often virtual and geographically dispersed. Branding consultants William Arruda and Kirsten Dixson observe, "Your personal brand must be powerful enough to impact colleagues and managers even when you are not physically present. The freedom allows you to work from anywhere at times that are convenient for you. But now you have to ensure that you're communicating your value with every e-mail and every phone call."[22] Knowing your brand also may simplify the lattice's many options.

Mark-to-Market Strategies

- **Take an outside-in approach to development.** Grow skills that are market relevant. To do that, keep your eyes on the horizon as well as on the road.

- **Seek out feedback from those around you.** Being open to constructive criticism is vital to continual learning.

- **Grow connections sideways, up, down, and out.** Developing relationships and networks benefits both the individual and the organization.

- **Manage your reputation online and offline.** You need to stand out in a crowd of standouts.

Having identified what makes you distinctive and how you add value gives you a true north around which to navigate your continued development. Jim Friedel held positions in five areas of Northwest Airlines over seventeen years, but there was a common thread as he sought to build his brand. "I wanted to be known as someone who could step into any situation, break it down into logical pieces, and explain to others what needed to be done," he explains.[23]

Friedel's focus on clear, strategic thinking and implementation led to successful work in finance, reservations, and marketing before he was tapped to evaluate the airline's ailing cargo division and ultimately led its turnaround. Although he spent almost eleven years in the cargo division, Friedel remained true to his intended brand—a strategic thinker rather than a "cargo guy." When he ultimately moved out of cargo, it was to a position consistent with the brand he had targeted and cultivated: he was picked to run strategic planning, which included the analysis of Northwest's merger with Delta Air Lines.

Although your brand is instrumental in garnering new opportunities and providing entrées into career-enhancing networks, its power can be just as influential in terms of what you *do not* get involved with. Wearing multiple hats and reporting to others in dotted-line relationships, for example, are prevalent in lattice organizations, and companies are offering up varied means to participate in all kinds of activities, from shaping strategy to improving processes. As a result, in the lattice world there are more occasions to make yourself known.

But getting involved at a cursory level across many areas can result in your having too little time to distinguish yourself in any single way. That's what one middle-level employee we'll call Edward learned the hard way. A skilled manager with high potential, Edward was invited to participate in and lead prominent committees and initiatives. Thinking that each would contribute to building his network and brand, he was reluctant to decline any offer. Although he made contributions to each, he spent so much of his time participating across multiple areas that he did not have time to make a noticeable and extraordinary contribution to any of them. This strategy wound up working counter to his brand-building efforts: he became known as someone who did not add substantial value.

The lesson? In a demanding environment, using the power of your brand to focus your efforts is as important as creating the opportunities to build and reinforce your brand.

OPTIMIZE CAREER–LIFE FIT

In our view, *work–life balance* is an unfortunate phrase, because it connotes a sense of opposing forces—work *versus* life. In reality, career and life are intertwined, and they need to be considered in tandem.

Despite the shortcomings of the term, the notion behind work–life balance is among the core elements of managing talent in most companies. It is so well established that the business press has columns devoted to topics within the realm of what we call career–life fit. *BusinessWeek*'s "Life Management" column, the *Wall Street Journal*'s "Work and Family" and "The Juggle" columns, and even CNN's Work/Life Balance Calculator serve as examples that fitting work into life and life into work is a mainstream business theme.

The opportunity for individuals is that lattice organizations offer more options for customizing how career and life come together. The challenge is that each alternative has benefits and trade-offs, so you need to take responsibility for choosing how career and life fit together for you personally at each moment in time, understanding that what is optimal at one career stage may not be at the next.

Engineers frequently need to juggle multiple objectives when they design products. For example, truck buyers typically want a suspension system that is durable, smooth riding, and cost-effective. Unfortunately, it is virtually impossible to maximize all three objectives at once. The most durable suspension is likely to be one that handles stiffly and weighs more, and that compromises fuel economy. The smoothest-riding suspension is less durable, and the cost to repair or replace it may outweigh any fuel savings that may come from a lower weight. The most cost-effective design in terms of fuel consumption is not likely to be the most durable or have the smoothest ride. Of the combinations, the most efficient choice maximizes two objectives to attain a given level of the third. Truck buyers must decide the mix of these dimensions that works best for them.

Similarly, individuals trade off among different objectives with respect to their careers, their home lives, their friends, their community efforts, and other dimensions as they strive to achieve their model of success. Following are real-life scenarios of three individuals whose stories illustrate the increasingly commonplace decisions individuals are making.

- Allen, a gifted forty-year-old analyst, is a respected player both inside the organization and within the financial community. He makes a fine living, but he does not have his eye on his boss's job, larger paychecks, or fatter bonuses. What he really wants is more personal days off so that he can work at his second love, performing in a jazz trio. For years now, he has been rewarded with additional paid time off in lieu of incremental cash compensation. It's a big reason he is still with the company.

- A twenty-seven-year-old high performer named Carolyn was recently offered a midlevel role—and turned it down. The proposed position would have increased her responsibilities and budget considerably, but she felt it wouldn't help her learn and develop new skills. Concerned about getting locked into a position that might not maximize her long-term employability options, Carolyn contemplated waiting until the right job opened up. She was willing to trade off less responsibility now for a future opportunity that would provide greater breadth.

- Steve is a fifty-five-year-old senior executive who has enjoyed a traditional career in many respects. Always on the move, he has built a series of successful businesses within his organization. But now, ten years from retirement, he wants to scale back his travel and spend more time with his partner and his grandchildren, even though the decision may limit his opportunities for further leadership roles. Like Allen and Carolyn, Steve is thinking about trade-offs and their future implications.

At a time when the interests, backgrounds, and family structures of employees are more varied than ever before, employees are by default more conscious of their career–life needs. By recognizing trade-offs and communicating your needs and preferences, you maximize your ability to make decisions that are optimal for you and your employer. If you are silent, unsure, or unwilling to talk about what success means to you, you hinder the ability of the organization to work with you to craft a solution that works for both parties.

Carol Carpenter serves as an example of an executive who has weighed many options to arrive at a career–life fit that works best for her and her family. Carpenter has what is sometimes referred to as an extreme job. She is general manager of consumer and small business products for Internet security firm TrendMicro. With the company's chief executive officer in California, the chief technology officer in Germany, the chief financial officer in Japan, and development teams in Asia, TrendMicro is a transnational company facing all the challenges you would expect of such a dispersed management structure.

At this stage of her career, Carpenter has optimized the various elements of her work and life. She speaks with great excitement about the company and her role, relating that she wakes up each weekday morning looking forward to what lies ahead. When asked about her balance between work and life, she laughs and at first says, "I have none."[24] But the more she talks, the more clear it becomes that she has found an optimal career–life fit for this point in time.

Her general manager role at a global company involves international travel, which pulls her away from her working husband and two children. However, when she is home—and she recently grounded herself for a month—she handles morning school drop-offs and largely blocks off 6 p.m. to 9 p.m. as family time. She handles e-mail and conference calls with Asia after 9 p.m. and gets up early to do the same with her European colleagues. Travel aside, she refuses to commute more than thirty minutes to the office and has no interest in pursuing positions that involve longer commutes or relocation. It is hectic, it is busy—but it all works.

Ten years ago, when her first child was an infant, a different mix of career and life was optimal. Her husband continued to work full-time, and Carpenter took a year off to spend time with the baby. She consulted for technology companies and venture capital firms during that period of her life, keeping current on trends and easing her transition back into full-time work.

Carpenter's story illustrates the key factors in optimizing career–life fit. She moves creatively between work and family responsibilities when not traveling, and she has created a self-imposed break from travel to recharge and reconnect. She has adjusted her mix of work and life over time as her circumstances have changed. And she has found an arrangement that provides mutual benefit to her and her employer. She stays engaged and productive because she is fulfilling her model of success.

An awareness of which aspects of careers and life are important to you puts you in a good position to pair your needs with your employer's while also keeping you energized. Unlike in the ladder world, where anything not work-related was largely considered irrelevant within the corporate bounds, integrating work with life in the lattice world helps you bring your full, productive self to the organization.

This requires a high level of trust and transparency: you need to trust your employer not to judge your commitment or competence by your life needs, and your employer needs to trust you to understand the organization's goals and customize how work is done to achieve them. Both sides partner to find what we call the "high water mark" of worker engagement and organizational results.

Ladder models are giving way to lattice ones. So whether you are an individual contributor or an executive, this change entails more personal responsibility and active choice. Navigating the corporate lattice requires that you take an options-oriented approach

Career–Life Fit Strategies

- **Think "over time" rather than "fixed point in time."** Recognize that choices can and likely will change. An individual might dial up to take advantage of a unique stretch opportunity and subsequently throttle down somewhat in conjunction with a life event. Integrating career with life is the proverbial marathon and not a sprint. Thinking about how your career will progress over time rather than at a particular point in time can maximize your overall long-term success.

- **Focus on mutual benefit.** Lopsided arrangements are usually short-lived, so maintain a spirit of collaboration and compromise. Sustainable options benefit both you and your employer.

- **Ride the wave.** New advances in careers, work, and participation shift up the curve of optimal outcomes, and radically new customization approaches give you and your employer more of what you both require.

---

to growth and development, mark to market your individual assets, and collaborate with employers to create an optimal career–life fit.

Over the past few decades, both the rate at which market leaders topple and the level of competitive intensity have doubled.[25] It used to be that 60 percent of corporate value creation depended on hard assets. Now, more than 85 percent relies on the intangible assets of people, brand, and intellectual property.[26] This shift places a higher stake on an organization's ability to engage its people. Continuing to invest for the future using yesterday's hard-coded corporate ladder blueprint is futile.

In this book, we've contrasted the characteristics of the industrial era corporate ladder with that of an emerging knowledge era corporate lattice, describing the differences between these two metaphorically rich models. We've shown that the lattice isn't a hypothetical case; it's already on the horizon, and there are clear benefits for companies that intentionally evolve toward it.

All the research and observations we have gleaned in the development of this work can be distilled into one projection: the intersection between high performance and sustainable career–life fit is the battleground on which competitiveness in the talent marketplace will play out.

*High performanc*e refers to all the usual characteristics the term evokes, including extraordinary financial results, a commanding market share, a culture of innovation, and a portfolio of compelling products and services. What's new to the equation is the added dimension of *career–life fit.* The term refers to the attributes that individuals value, such as extraordinary growth and development, opportunities to make meaningful contributions, a sense of belonging and connection to a greater whole, the accomplishments each person delivers and takes pride in, and the ability to have all this and still have a life.

No longer relegated to the realm of the less ambitious or less committed nor defined as a women's work–life balance issue, career–life fit is the ability to find a sustainable, adaptive, and scalable way to fit life into work and work into life over time. And make no mistake about it: recognizing and adopting lattice ways to build careers, work, and participate are at the center of the equation.

The ladder belief that high performance and sustainable career–life fit are opposing forces must give way to a new reality: that they are mutually reinforcing and inextricably linked. While this concludes our tour of the lattice landscape, the journey is only beginning.

NOTES

CHAPTER 1

1. F. Warren McFarlan and Cathy Benko, "Managing a Growth Culture: How CEOs Can Initiate and Monitor a Successful Growth-Project Culture," *Strategy & Leadership* 32, no. 1 (2004): 34–42.

2. National Commission on Mathematics and Science Teaching for the 21st Century, *Before It's Too Late* (Washington, DC: U.S. Department of Education, September 2000), http://www.ed.gov/inits/Math/glenn/report.pdf.

3. U.S. Census Bureau, Housing and Household Economic Statistics Division, Fertility and Family Statistics Branch, *America's Families and Living Arrangements: 2007*, http://www.census.gov/population/www/socdemo/hh-fam/cps2007.html; Catalyst, *Two Careers, One Marriage: Making It Work in the Workplace* (New York: Catalyst, 1998).

4. Heather Boushey and Ann O'Leary, eds., *The Shriver Report: A Woman's Nation Changes Everything* (Washington, DC: Center for American Progress, 2009), 32; Bureau of Labor Statistics, *Current Employment Statistics (National)*, October 2009, tables B-3 and B-4, ftp://ftp.bls.gov/pub/suppl/empsit.ceseeb3.txt.

5. Ellen Galinsky, Kerstin Aumann, and James Bond, *Times Are Changing: Gender and Generation at Work and at Home: The 2008 Study of the Changing Workforce* (New York: Families and Work Institute, 2009), 23.

6. AARP, *What Older Workers Want From Work*, http://www.aarp.org/money/careers/employerresourcecenter/ trends/a2004-04-20-olderworkers.html; Lisa Belkin, "Teaching Office Decorum to the iPod Generation," *New York Times News Service*, August 2, 2007, http://www.marycrane.com/press/27-ChicagoTribune_08-02-07_Teaching%20Office%20Decorum.pdf.

7. Sam Roberts, "In a Generation, Minorities May Be the U.S. Majority," *New York Times*, August 13, 2008, http://www.nytimes.com/2008/08/14/washington/14census.html?scp=2&sq=majority%20minority&st=cse.

8. Cathy Benko and Anne Weisberg, *Mass Career Customization* (Boston: Harvard Business School Press, 2007). Mass Career Customization and MCC are trademarks and service marks of Deloitte Development LLC.

9. Watson Wyatt, *Driving Business Results Through Continuous Engagement, 2008/2009 WorkUSA Survey Report* 4 (New York: Watson Wyatt, February 3, 2009).

10. Towers Perrin, *Closing the Engagement Gap: A Road Map for Driving Superior Business Performance, Towers Perrin Global Workforce Study 2007–2008*, TP531-08, http://www.towersperrin.com/tp/showhtml.jsp?url=global/publications/gws/index.htm&country=global.

11. Based on author research conducted from April 15 to April 30, 2009, on the Web sites of 2009 *Fortune* 100 Best Companies to Work For winners and advertising activity research conducted by Video Monitoring Service.

12. Alex Edmans, "Does the Stock Market Fully Value Intangibles? Employee Satisfaction and Equity Prices," MIT Working Paper (Cambridge, MA: MIT, 2007), http://finance.wharton.upenn.edu/~aedmans/Rowe%20Summary.pdf.

13. Parnassus Investments Web site, http://www.parnassus.com/parnassus-mutual-funds/workplace/Performance.aspx.

14. David Shadovitz, "Investing in Workplace Excellence," *Human Resource Executive Online*, May 18, 2009, http://www.hreonline.com/HRE/story.jsp?storyId=211576886.

15. Interview with Gwen McDonald, senior vice president human resources, and Grace Soriano-Abad, senior director, global staffing, NetApp, by Molly Anderson, Suzanne Kounkel, and Laura Stokker, August 3, 2009.

16. Corporate Executive Board Staff, "The Increasing Call for Work-Life Balance," *BusinessWeek*, March 27, 2009, http://www.businessweek.com/managing/content/mar2009/ca20090327_734197.htm.

17. Catalyst, *Two Careers, One Marriage*.

18. "Number of Jobs Held, Labor Market Activity, and Earnings Growth Among the Youngest Baby Boomers: Results from a Longitudinal Survey Summary," Bureau of Labor Statistics press release, June 27, 2008, http://www.bls.gov/news.release/nlsoy.nr0.htm.

19. Cathy Benko, "From Corporate Ladder to Corporate Lattice: Aligning the Workplace with Today's Non-Traditional Workforce Using Mass Career Customization," Taleo Corporation Web seminar, June 25, 2009, https://taleo.webex.com/taleo/lsr.php?AT=pb&SP=EC&rID=52132972&rKey=6994C8171BAAEB75.

20. Discussion with Betsy Rafael, vice president of finance for a consumer technology company, by Cathy Benko, May 5, 2009, and follow-up interviews by Cathy Benko, June 18, 2009, and by Cathy Benko and Molly Anderson, August 20, 2009.

21. Interview with Tanya Clemons, senior vice president and chief talent officer, Pfizer, by Cathy Benko and Laura Stokker, June 26, 2009.

22. Michael Gadd, "More Workers Telecommuting," Inc.com, August 28, 2008, http://www.inc.com/news/articles/2008/08/telecommuting.html.

23. Interview with Ellen Galinsky, president, Families and Work Institute, by Suzanne MacGibbon and Anne Weisberg, June 26, 2009, citing *2008 National Study of the Changing Workforce* (New York: Families and Work Institute, 2008). For similar findings, see WFD Consulting, *Innovative Workplace Flexibility Options for Hourly Workers* (Washington, DC: Corporate Voices for Working Families, 2009); Boston College Center for Work and Family, *Measuring the Impact of Workplace Flexibility* (Boston: Boston College, 2000).

24. Discussion with Maggie Wilderotter, chairman and CEO, Frontier Communications, with Cathy Benko, December 17, 2009.

25. Interview with Elizabeth Bryant, senior director of talent development, and Brian Lusk, manager of online relationships and special projects, Southwest Airlines, by Molly Anderson and Laura Stokker, June 23, 2009.

26. Thomas Friedman, *The World Is Flat* (New York: Farrar, Straus, and Giroux, 2005), 204.

27. Linda Cureton, "NASA Goddard Space Flight Center Launches Spacebook," *NASA Goddard CIO Blog*, June 12, 2009, http://blogs.nasa.gov/cm/blog/Goddard-CIO-Blog.blog/posts/post_1244861198431.html.

28. Noam Cohen, "Care to Write Army Doctrine? With ID, Log On," *New York Times*, August 13, 2009, http://www.nytimes.com/2009/08/14/business/14army.html?scp=6&sq=Army&st=cse.

29. Padmasree Warrior, "Cisco Point of View on Cloud Computing," *The Platform: Opinions and Insights from Cisco*, July 8, 2009, http://blogs.cisco.com/news/comments/cisco_point_of_view_on_cloud_computing/.

30. Ed Lawler, *Talent: Making People Your Competitive Advantage* (San Francisco: Jossey-Bass, 2008), 86.

31. Interview with David Turner, executive vice president and chief financial officer, Thomson Reuters Markets, by Cathy Benko and Molly Anderson, September 29, 2009.

32. Clay Shirky, *Here Comes Everybody: The Power of Organizing Without Organizations* (New York: Penguin Press, 2008).

33. Douglas Elmendorf, Gregory Mankiw, and Lawrence H. Summers, *Brookings Papers on Economic Activity: Spring 2008* (Washington, DC: Brookings Institution Press, 2008).

34. Interview with John Hagel III and John Seely Brown by Cathy Benko, Molly Anderson, and Suzanne Kounkel MacGibbon, May 11, 2009, with follow-up discussions by Cathy Benko, July 20 and 21, 2009.

CHAPTER 2

1. Bryant Ott, "Investors Take Note: Engagement Boosts Earnings," *Gallup Management Journal*, June 14, 2007, http://gmj.gallup.com/content/27799/investors-take-note-engagement-boosts-earnings.aspx.

2. Watson Wyatt, *Driving Results Through Continuous Engagement: 2008/2009 WorkUSA Survey Report* (New York: Watson Wyatt, February 3, 2009), 4.

3. *Employee Engagement: Stories of Success* (Brisbane, Australia: JRA, November 2008), http://www.jra.co.nz/storiesofsuccess.aspx.

4. "Tough Decisions in a Downturn Don't Have to Lead to Disengaged Employees," *BusinessWire*, August 14, 2009, http://www.businesswire.com/news/google/20090812006251/en.

5. Maggie Ozan-Rafferty, "Hospitals: Never Have a Never Event: How Engagement Can Reduce Error Rates in Healthcare Organizations," *Gallup Management Journal*, May 7, 2009, http://gmj.gallup.com/content/118255/ Hospitals-Event.aspx.

6. "Understanding the True Cost of Disengagement," *Hewitt Quarterly Asia Pacific*, July 2007, http://www.hewittassociates.com/Intl/AP/en-AP/Knowledge Center/Magazine/HQ_18/articles/cost-disaggrement.html.

7. Watson Wyatt/World at Work, *Looking Toward Recovery: Realigning Rewards and Reengaging Employees: The 2009/2010 U.S. Strategic Rewards Report* (New York: Watson Wyatt, 2009), 8.

8. Heather Boushey and Ann O'Leary, eds., *The Shriver Report: A Woman's Nation Changes Everything* (Washington, DC: Center for American Progress, 2009), 17.

9. Monique Gougisha and Amanda Stout, "We Are Family: Employees with Family Responsibilities Are Insisting on Equal Treatment, and Are Finding Supportive Voices in Court," *HR Magazine*, April 2007, http://findarticles.com/p/articles/mi_m3495/is_4_52/ai_n19039028/.

10. MetLife Mature Market Institute/National Alliance for Caregiving, *The MetLife Caregiving Cost Study: Productivity Losses to U.S. Business* (Westport, CT: MetLife, July 2006), 4.

11. Robert Marquand, "Family Ties Take New Shapes in a Prosperous China," *Christian Science Monitor*, December 16, 2004, http://www.csmonitor.com/2004/1216/p10s01-woap.html.

12. Saritha Rai, "Senior Moment," *Forbes Asia*, September 15, 2008, http://www.forbes.com/global/2008/0915/064.html.

13. Ellen Galinsky, James Bond, and Kelly Sakai, *2008 National Study of Employers* (New York: Families and Work Institute, 2009), 10.

14. Casey Mulligan, "A Milestone for Working Women?" Economix blog, *New York Times*, January 14, 2009, http://economix.blogs.nytimes.com/2009/01/14/a-milestone-for-women-workers/; Casey Mulligan, "What Explains the 'Mancession'?" Economix blog, *New York Times*, September 30, 2009, http://economix.blogs.nytimes.com/2009/09/30/what-explains-the-mancession/.

15. International Labour Office, *Global Employment Trends for Women*, March 2008, http://www.ilo.org/wcmsp5/groups/public/---dgreports/---dcomm/documents/publication/wcms_091225.pdf.

16. U.S. Department of Education, National Center for Education Statistics, *Digest of Education Statistics* (Washington, DC: U.S. Department of Education, 2007), Table 258, http://nces.ed.gov/Programs/digest/d07/tables/xls/tabn258.xls.

17. Eurostat, "Share of Women Among Tertiary Students," June 2008, http://epp.eurostat.ec.europa.eu/tgm/table.do?tab=table&init=1&plugin=1&language=en&pcode=tps00063.

18. Nazila Fathi, "Starting at Home, Iran's Women Fight for Rights," *New York Times*, February 13, 2009.

19. Ellen Galinsky, Kerstin Aumann, and James Bond, *Times Are Changing: Gender and Generation at Work and at Home: The 2008 Study of the Changing Workforce* (New York: Families and Work Institute, 2009), 1.

20. Ibid., 2.

21. Marianne Bertrand, Claudia Goldin, and Lawrence F. Katz, "Dynamics of the Gender Gap for Young Professionals in the Financial and Corporate Sectors," NBER working paper 14681, National Bureau of Economic Research, Cambridge, MA, January 2009, 30.

22. Galinsky, Aumann, and Bond, *Times Are Changing*, 9.

23. Ibid., 8.

24. Oriel Sullivan and Scott Coltrane, "Men's Changing Contribution to Housework and Child Care" (discussion paper prepared for the 11th annual conference of the Council on Contemporary Families, University of Illinois, Chicago,

April 25–26, 2002), http://www.contemporaryfamilies.org/subtemplate.php?t=briefingPapers&ext=menshousework.

25. Ibid.

26. American Business Collaboration, *The New Career Paradigm: Attracting and Retaining Critical Talent* (Newton, MA: WFD Consulting, 2006), 7.

27. Michael Kimmel, "Has a Man's World Become a Woman's Nation?" in Boushey and O'Leary, eds., *The Shriver Report: A Woman's Nation Changes Everything,* 355.

28. "Nearly One-Half of Working Dads Would Relinquish Breadwinner Role to Spend More Time with Their Kids, According to CareerBuilder.com's Annual Father's Day Survey," CareerBuilder.com, June 14, 2005, http://www.careerbuilder.com/share/aboutus/pressreleasesdetail.aspx?id=pr178&sd=6%2f14%2f2005&ed=12%2f31%2f2005&siteid=cbpr&sc_cmp1=cb_pr178_.

29. "Fewer Working Fathers Willing to Be Stay-At-Home Dads Than Previous Years, Finds CareerBuilder's Annual Father's Day Survey," CareerBuilder.com, June 17, 2009, http://www.careerbuilder.com/share/aboutus/pressreleasesdetail.aspx?id=pr502&sd=6/17/2009&ed=06/17/2009.

30. Peter Cappelli, *Talent on Demand: Managing Talent in an Age of Uncertainty* (Boston: Harvard Business School Press, 2008), 43.

31. Daniel Quinn Mills and G. Bruce Friesen, *Broken Promises: An Unconventional View of What Went Wrong at IBM* (Boston: Harvard Business School Press, 1996), 97.

32. Raghuram Rajan and Julie Wulf, "The Flattening Firm: Evidence from Panel Data on the Changing Nature of Corporate Hierarchies," National Bureau of Economic Research Working Paper Series, Working Paper #9633, April 2003, http://www.nber.org/papers/w9633.

33. Himanshu Juneja, "Ideal Span of Control in an Organization," December 31, 2008, http://www.articleclick.com/Article/Ideal-Span-of-Control-in-an-organization/1078645.

34. Thomas L. Friedman, *The World Is Flat* (New York: Picador, 2007).

35. Oren Harari, "Imperatives for Deflating the Fat Organization," *Management Review* 81, no. 6 (1992): 61.

36. Capelli, *Talent on Demand,* 71.

37. Quoted in Miawling Lam, "Better Ways to Nurture Talent," *Sunday Telegraph,* February 17, 2008, http://www.news.com.au/business/business-smarts/sideways-promotion-keeps-staff/story-e6frfma9-1111115578718.

38. Bureau of Labor Statistics, "Economic News Release," November 6, 2009, Table A-4, http://www.bls.gov/news.release/empsit.t04.htm; Bureau of Labor Statistics, "Economic News Release," November 6, 2009, Table A-1, http://www.bls.gov/news.release/empsit.t01.htm.

39. Peter Coy, "Help Wanted: Why That Sign's Bad," *BusinessWeek,* April 30, 2009, http://www.businessweek.com/magazine/content/09_19/b4130040117561.htm.

40. *2009 Talent Shortage Survey Results,* Manpower Inc., May 2009, 1, http://files.shareholder.com/downloads/MAN/787752987x0x297372/dab9f206-75f4-40b7-88fb-3ca81333140f/09TalentShortage_Results_USLetter_FINAL_FINAL.pdf.

41. IBM, *Unlocking the DNA of the Adaptable Workforce: The IBM Global Human Capital Study* (Armonk, New York: IBM, 2008), 30.

42. "Capturing Talent: Asia's Skills Shortage," *Economist,* August 18, 2007.

43. Norman R. Augustine, *Is America Falling Off the Flat Earth?* National Academy of Sciences, National Academy of Engineering, Institute of Medicine (Washington, D.C.: National Academies Press, 2007), http://www.nap.edu/openbook.php?record_id=12021&page=37.

44. McKinsey & Co, Social Sector Office, *The Economic Impact of the Achievement Gap in America's Schools* (New York: McKinsey & Company, April 2009), 6.

45. Tamara Erickson, *Retire Retirement* (Boston: Harvard Business School Press, 2008), 42.

46. M. J. Stephey, "Gen-X: The Ignored Generation," *Time,* April 16, 2008, http://www.time.com/time/arts/article/0,8599,1731528,00.html; Sylvia Ann Hewlett, Laura Sherbin, and Karen Sumberg, "How Gen Y and Boomers Will Reshape Your Agenda," *Harvard Business Review* (July–August 2009), 123.

47. Population Division of the Department of Economic and Social Affairs of the United Nations Secretariat, "World Population Prospects: The 2008 Revision," http://esa.un.org/unpp.

48. Council of the European Union, "Council Adopts the 'EU Blue Card': More Advantages for High-Skilled Foreign Workers," May 25, 2009, http://www.consilium.europa.eu/ueDocs/cms_Data/docs/pressdata/en/misc/107989.pdf; Bailey Somers, "Skilled Labor Shortage Breeds EU Blue Card," Employment Law 360, Portfolio Media, October 24, 2007, http://www.hunton.com/files/tbl_s10News%5CFile Upload44%5C14746%5CEU_BlueCard.pdf.

49. Erickson, *Retire Retirement.*

50. AARP, "About AARP," http://www.aarp.org/aarp/About_AARP/; see also, for example, Eric D. Beinhocker, Diana Farrell, and Ezra Greenberg, "Why Baby Boomers Will Need to Live Longer," *McKinsey Quarterly,* November 2008; David DeLong & Associates, *Living Longer, Working Longer: The Changing Landscape of the Aging Workforce* (New York: MetLife Mature Market Institute, 2006); Brad Edmondson, "Working Wonders," *AARP Magazine,* November/December 2005; AARP, *Staying Ahead of the Curve 2003: The AARP Working in Retirement Study* (Washington, DC: AARP, 2003).

51. Families and Work Institute, *Gender and Generation in the Workplace: An Issues Brief* (New York: Families and Work Institute, 2006).

52. Deloitte Research, *Generation Y: Powerhouse of the Global Economy* (New York: Deloitte Development LLC, 2009).

53. Andrew Canter and Craig Segall, general letter to U.S. law firms, April 2, 2007, http://online.wsj.com/public/resources/documents/lawfirm0403.pdf.

54. "The 'Trophy Kids' Go to Work," *Wall Street Journal,* October 21, 2008, adapted from Ron Alsop, *The Trophy Kids Grow Up: How the Millennial Generation Is Shaking Up the Workplace* (Hoboken, NJ: Jossey-Bass, 2008), http://online.wsj.com/article/SB122455219391652725.html.

55. John Hagel III, John Seely Brown, and Lang Davison, *Measuring the Forces of Long-Term Change: The 2009 Shift Index* (San Jose, CA: Deloitte Center for the Edge, 2009), 26–29, http://www.deloitte.com/assets/Dcom-UnitedStates/Local%20Assets/Documents/us_tmt_ce_ShiftIndex_072109ecm.pdf.

56. *The Internet Big Picture: World Internet Users and Population Stats* (Bogota, Colombia: Miniwatts Marketing Group, September 30, 2009), http://internetworldstats.com/stats.htm.

57. WorldAtWork, *Telework Trendlines 2009* (Scottsdale, AZ: February 2009), 6, http://www.worldatwork.org/waw/adimLink?id=31115; and Bureau of Labor

Statistics, "The Employment Situation: December 2008," January 9, 2009, 2, http://www.bls.gov/news.release/archives/empsit_01092009.pdf.

58. Stephen Drake et al., *Worldwide Mobile Worker Population 2007–2011 Forecast* (Framingham, MA: IDC, March 2008).

59. Louis van Wyk Auckland, "JetBlue's Reservations Staff Embrace Teleworking," *Computerworld*, November 20, 2008, http://computerworld.co.nz/news.nsf/netw/8D7C8DD2280E318FCC257504000C2BF7.

60. Chuck Salter, "Calling JetBlue," *Fast Company*, December 19, 2007, http://www.fastcompany.com/magazine/82/jetblue_agents.html.

61. Auckland, "JetBlue's Reservations Staff Embrace Teleworking."

62. Salter, "Calling JetBlue."

63. Mark Zuckerberg, "An Open Letter from Facebook Founder Mark Zuckerberg," http://blog.facebook.com/blog.php?post=190423927130; Ben Parr, "Facebook Now Has Over 300 Million Users," http://mashable.com/2009/09/15/facebook-300-million/; "Social Media Stats: MySpace Music Growing, Twitter's Big Move," July 17, 2009, http://blog.nielsen.com/nielsenwire/online_mobile/social-media-stats-myspace-music-growing-twitters-big-move/.

64. U.S. Census Bureau, Population Division, *Annual Estimates of the Resident Population by Sex, Race, and Hispanic Origin for the United States: April 1, 2000 to July 1, 2008*, NC-EST2008-03 (Washington, DC: U.S. Census Bureau, May 14, 2009), http://www.census.gov/popest/national/asrh/NC-EST2008-srh.html.

65. "An Older and More Diverse Nation by Midcentury," press release, U.S. Census Bureau News, August 14, 2008, http://www.census.gov/Press-Release/www/releases/archives/population/012496.html.

66. "More Than 300 Counties Now 'Majority-Minority,'" press release, U.S. Census Bureau News, August 9, 2007, http://www.census.gov/Press-Release/www/releases/archives/population/010482.html.

67. Hope Yen, "Multi-Racial Americans Become Fastest Growing Group," *Huffington Post*, May 28, 2009, http://www.huffingtonpost.com/2009/05/29/multiracial-americans-bec_n_208989.html.

68. Sam Roberts, "In a Generation, Minorities May Be the U.S. Majority," *New York Times*, August 13, 2008, http://www.nytimes.com/2008/08/14/washington/14census.html?scp=2&sq=majority%20minority&st=cse.

69. Treasury Board of Canada Secretariat, "Citizenship and Immigration Canada," February 12, 2008, http://www.tbs-sct.gc.ca/rpp/2008-2009/inst/imc/imc01-eng.asp.

70. DeAnne Aguirre, Sylvia Ann Hewlett, and Laird Post, *Global Talent Innovation Strategies for Breakthrough Performance* (New York: Booz & Company, 2009), 3.

71. Stanley Davis, *Future Perfect* (New York: Addison Wesley, 1987); Joseph Pine II, *Mass Customization: The New Frontier in Business Competition* (Boston: Harvard Business School Press, 1992).

72. Mrinal Ghosh, Shantanu Dutta, and Stefan Stremersch, "Customizing Complex Products: When Should the Vendor Take Control?" *Journal of Marketing Research* 43 (November 2006): 664–679.

73. Interview with Cynthia Heckmann, retired chief human capital officer, and Carol Willett, retired chief learning officer, Government Accountability Office, by Cathy Benko and Molly Anderson, July 23, 2009.

74. Deloitte Research, *It's 2008: Do You Know Where Your Talent Is?* (New York: Deloitte Development LLC, 2007).

75. Interview with Mary Petrovich, CEO, AxleTech International, by Cathy Benko, May 30, 2009.

76. Ryan Healy, comment on "Twentysomething: Why I Don't Want Work/Life Balance," Brazen Careerist Online Community, comment posted April 3, 2009, http://blog.penelopetrunk.com/2007/04/02/twentysomething-why-i-dont-want-worklife-balance/.

77. Jill Arlinghaus, comment on "Models of Success," Cathy Benko's Blog, posted May 5, 2009, https://www.deloittenet.com/AboutDeloitte/People_Community/DEN/SearchDStreet/default.htm?page=https%3A%2F%2Fsearch%2Edeloittenet%2Ecom%2FPages%2Fpeopleresults%2Easpx%3Fk%3Dcathy%20benko.

CHAPTER 3

1. Interview with Mike Davis, senior vice president, global human resources, and Kevin Wilde, chief learning officer, General Mills, by Cathy Benko and Laura Stokker, June 15, 2009.

2. Tom Peters, "The Brand Called You," *Fast Company*, August 1997, http://www.fastcompany.com/magazine/10/brandyou.html.

3. A. G. Watts, "Reshaping Career Development for the 21st Century" (inaugural professorial lecture at the University of Derby, Centre for Guidance Studies, Derby, United Kingdom, December 8, 1998), 2.

4. See, for instance, Brad Harrington and Douglas T. Hall, *Career Management & Work-Life Integration: Using Self-Assessment to Navigate Contemporary Careers* (Thousand Oaks, CA: Sage Publications, 2007); Michael B. Arthur and Denise M. Rousseau, *The Boundaryless Career: A New Employment Principle for a New Organizational Era* (New York: Oxford University Press, 1996); Sherry E. Sullivan and Lisa A. Mainiero, "Kaleidoscope Careers: Benchmarking Ideas for Fostering Family-Friendly Workplaces," *Organizational Dynamics* 36, no. 1 (2007): 45–62.

5. Comment on "Employee Loyalty Isn't Gone, It's Just Different," Penelope Trunk's Brazen Careerist, comment posted April 29, 2007, http://blog.penelopetrunk.com/2007/04/29/employee-loyalty-isnt-gone-its-just-different.

6. Corporate Executive Board Staff, "The Increasing Call for Work-Life Balance," *BusinessWeek*, March 27, 2009, http://www.businessweek.com/managing/content/mar2009/ca20090327_734197.htm.

7. Brian Amble, "Work-Life Balance Becoming Critical to Recruitment and Retention," *Management-Issues*, February 1, 2006, http://www.management-issues.com/2006/8/24/research/work-life-balance-becoming-critical-to-recruitment-and-retention.asp.

8. Henry Faber, "Employment Insecurity: The Decline in Worker-Firm Attachment in the United States," working paper 530, Industrial Relations Section, Princeton University, Princeton, NJ, July 2008.

9. Employee Benefit Research Institute, *History of 401(k) Plans: An Update* (Washington, DC: EBRI, February 2005), http://www.ebri.org/pdf/publications/facts/0205fact.a.pdf.

10. U.S. Bureau of Labor Statistics, *Retirement Benefits: Access, Participation, and Take-Up Rates, Private Industry Workers, National Compensation Survey* (Washington, DC: BLS, March 2009), 165, http://www.bls.gov/ncs/ebs/benefits/2009/ebbl0044.pdf.

11. Brian Kropp and Tiffany Fountain, "The Fraying Employment Contract," *BusinessWeek*, October 13, 2009, http://www.businessweek.com/managing/content/oct2009/ca20091013_407300.htm.

12. Aspen Institute, *Where Will They Lead? MBA Student Attitudes About Business & Society* (Washington, CD: Center for Business Education, 2008) http://www.aspeninstitute.org/sites/default/files/content/docs/business%20and%20society%20program/SAS_PRINT_FINAL. PDF.

13. Anne Fisher, "Want a New Job? Give Your Old One a Makeover," *Fortune*, January 5, 2007, http://money.cnn.com/2007/01/03/news/economy/annie_newjob.fortune/index.htm.

14. Leigh Branham, *The Seven Hidden Reasons Employees Leave* (Washington, DC: ASAE and the Center for Association Leadership), February 2005, http://www.asaecenter.org/PublicationsResources/EUArticle.cfm?ItemNumber=11514.

15. Ron Alsop, *The Trophy Kids Grow Up* (San Francisco: Jossey-Bass, 2008), 36.

16. Penelope Trunk, "Motivating Gen Y in a Downturn," *BusinessWeek*, June 9, 2009, http://www.businessweek.com/managing/content/jun2009/ca2009069_851860.htm?chan=rss_topEmailedStories_ssi_5.

17. Towers Perrin, *Closing the Engagement Gap: A Road Map for Driving Superior Business Performance, Towers Perrin Global Workforce Study 2007–2008*, TP531-08 (New York: 2007), http://www.biworldwide.com/info/pdf/Towers_Perrin_Global_Workforce_ Study.pdf.

18. Rebecca Thorman, "How to Innovate Your Career," Modite blog, comment posted July 30, 2009, http://modite.com/blog/2009/07/30/how-to-innovate-your-career/.

19. Interchange Group, *6 Strategies for Engaging Generation X* (Los Angeles: Interchange Group, 2007), http://www.interchange-group.com/data/6%20Strategies%20for%20Engaging%20Generation%20X.pdf.

20. Anne Fisher, "Are You Stuck in Middle Management Hell?" *Fortune*, August 15, 2009, http://money.cnn.com/magazines/fortune/fortune_archive/2006/08/21/8383654/index.htm.

21. Sylvia Ann Hewlett et al., *Bookend Generations: Leveraging Talent and Finding Common Ground* (New York: Center for Work-Life Policy, July 2009), http://www.worklifepolicy.org/index.php/section/research_pubs.

22. Mercer, *Employers Expect Training Investments to Grow Faster Than Investments in Other HR Categories* (New York: Mercer, October 2, 2007), http://www.mercer.com/summary.htm?siteLanguage=100&idContent=1282915.

23. Interview with Tamar Elkeles, vice president of learning and development, QUALCOMM, by Laura Stokker, May 11, 2009, and correspondence with Molly Anderson, January 3, 2010.

24. American Society for Training and Development, *2005 State of the Industry Report* (Alexandria, VA: ASTD), 2005, http://www.astd.org; American Society for Training and Development, *2008 State of the Industry Report* (Alexandria, VA: 2008), http://www.astd.org.

25. Trunk, "Motivating Gen Y in a Downturn."

26. Morgan McCall, Michael Lombardo, and Ann Morrison, *The Lessons of Experience: How Successful Executives Develop on the Job* (Lexington, MA: Lexington Books, 1988).

27. General Electric career Web site, http://www.ge.com/company/culture/leadership_learning.html.

28. James Maxwell, "Work System Design to Improve the Economic Performance of the Firm," *Business Process Management Journal* 14, no. 3 (2008): 432–446.

29. Gregory Smith, *401 Proven Ways to Retain Your Best Employees* (Atlanta: Chart Your Course International, 2007), 76.

30. Fisher, "Are You Stuck in Middle Management Hell?"

31. Ibid.

32. U.S. Congress, *Interagency Aerospace Revitalization Task Force*, Public Law 109-420, December 20, 2006.

33. Deloitte Research, *2009 Industry Outlook: Aerospace & Defense Challenging Times, Emerging Opportunities* (New York: Deloitte Development LLC, 2009).

34. Fisher, "Are You Stuck in Middle Management Hell?"

35. Ellen Galinsky, Kersten Auman, and James T. Bond, *Times Are Changing: Gender and Generation at Work and at Home, National Study of the Changing Workforce* (Berkeley, CA: Families and Work Institute, 2009), http://www.working-families.org/organize/pdf /Times_Are_Changing.pdf.

36. Hewlett et al., *Bookend Generations*.

37. Elizabeth Kelleher, *In Dual-Earner Couples, Family Roles Are Changing in U.S.* (Washington, DC: U.S. Department of State, March 21, 2007), http://www.america.gov/st/washfile-english/2007/March/20070321162913berehellek0.6708338.html. Heather Boushey and Ann O'Leary, eds., *The Shriver Report: A Woman's Nation Changes Everything* (Washington, DC: Center for American Progress, 2009), 32.

38. Knowledge@W. P. Carey, *Flexibility's Price Tag: Gain Time, Lose Career Footing* (Tempe, AZ: W. P. Carey School of Business, Arizona State University, February 14, 2007), http://knowledge.wpcarey.asu.edu/article.cfm?articleid=1371.

39. Aquent, The Tuck School of Business at Dartmouth, and Work + Life Fit Inc., *Changing the Career Ladder: Paving Flexible Pathways for Today's Talent* (Chicago: Aquent, January 2007), http://exec.tuck.dartmouth.edu/CustomerFiles_dartmouth/upload/upload/ TuckSurvey.pdf.

40. Knowledge@W. P. Carey, *Flexibility's Price Tag*.

41. Norma Jean Mattei and Lisa Jennings, "Pit Stops and Scenic Routes: How to Aid Women to Stay on Track in Their Careers," *Leadership and Management in Engineering* 8, no. 1 (2008): 28, http://www.asce.org/files/pdf/professional/diversity/ Mattei.pdf.

42. Sylvia Ann Hewlett and Carolyn Buck Luce, "On-Ramps and Off-Ramps: Keeping Talented Women on the Road to Success," *Harvard Business Review* 83, no. 3 (March 2005): 43–57, http://harvardbusiness.org/product/off-ramps-and-on-ramps-keeping-talented-women-on-t/an/R0503B-PDF-ENG.

43. American Institute of Certified Public Accountants, *Building Bridges: Strategies for a Successful Off-Ramping Program* (Durham, NC: AICPA, 2007), http://www.aicpa.org/download/career/wofi/0666-331_WLWIECs_Off-Ramping_Program.pdf.

44. Aquent et al., *Changing the Career Ladder*.

45. Civic Ventures and MetLife Foundation, *Encore Career Survey* (San Francisco: June 2008), http://www.civicventures.org/publications/surveys/encore_career_survey/Encore_Survey.pdf.

46. Sid Groeneman and Elizabeth Pope, *Staying Ahead of the Curve 2007: The AARP Work and Career Study* (Washington, DC: AARP, 2008), 13, 44, http://assets.aarp.org/rgcenter/econ/work_career_08.pdf.

47. Aquent et al., *Changing the Career Ladder*.

48. Workplace Options, *Work-Life Benefits Key to Employee Satisfaction, Retention During Economic Downturn* (Raleigh, NC: Workplace Options, May 5, 2009), http://www.workplaceoptions.com/news_PressArchives09.asp#.

49. Interview with Karla Walker, talent management consultant, American Family Insurance, by Molly Anderson, January 5, 2009, and by Laura Stokker, May 18, 2009.

50. Peter F. Drucker, "Knowledge Worker Productivity: The Biggest Challenge," *California Management Review* 4, no. 2 (Winter 1999): 79–94.

51. Thomas Davenport, *Thinking for a Living: How to Get Better Performance and Results from Knowledge Workers* (Boston: Harvard Business Press, 2005), http://common.books24x7.com/book/id_12479/book.asp.

52. Teppo Felin, Joshua Tomsik, and Todd Zenger, "The Knowledge Economy: Emerging Organizational Forms, Missing Microfoundations and Key Considerations for Managing Human Capital," *Human Resource Management* 48, no. 4 (July–August 2009): 555–570, http://www3.interscience.wiley.com/journal/122519825/abstract.

53. Interview with Mike Davis and Kevin Wilde, June 15, 2009.

54. Posting on "Appealing Technical Path Career Options," Stack Overflow Q&A site, comment posted November 5, 2008, http://stackoverflow.com/questions/267069/appealing-technical-career-path-options.

55. Karl Flinders, "Standard Life Keeps IT Fresh with Enthusiasm and Experience," *ComputerWeekly*, July 12, 2009, http://www.computerweekly.com/Articles/2009/07/07/236773/Standard-Life-keeps-IT-fresh-with-enthusiasm-and-experience.htm.

56. Robert Rosseter, *Nursing Shortage Fact Sheet* (Washington, DC: American Association of Colleges of Nurses, June 2009), http://www.aacn.nche.edu/Media/FactSheets/NursingShortage.htm.

57. *How Career Lattices Help Solve Nursing and Other Workforce Shortages in Healthcare: A Guide for Workforce Investment Boards, One-Stop Career Centers, Healthcare Employers, Industry Alliances, and Higher Education Providers* (Chicago: Council for Adult and Experiential Learning and the U.S. Department of Labor, June 2005), http://www.cael.org/pdf/publication_pdf/Career_Lattice_guidebook.pdf, 5.

58. Interview with Phyllis Snyder, vice president, Council for Adult and Experiential Learning, by Laura Stokker and Megan Farrell, May 18, 2009.

59. *How Career Lattices Help Solve Nursing and Other Workforce Shortages in Healthcare.* See also Rosseter, *Nursing Shortage Fact Sheet.*

60. Interview with Ralph Baxter, CEO, Orrick, Herrington, Sutcliffe LLP, by Cathy Benko and Molly Anderson, December, 17, 2009.

61. Interview with Katharine Crost, partner-in-charge, Orrick, Herrington, & Sutcliffe LLP, by Anne Weisberg and Laura Stokker, June 3, 2009.

62. Internal document, "Orrick's Talent Model: Your Future," 2009.

63. Interview with Laura Saklad, chief lawyer development officer, Orrick, Herrington, Sutcliffe LLP, by Cathy Benko and Molly Anderson, December, 17, 2009.

64. Interview with Ralph Baxter, December 17, 2009.

65. Cathleen Benko and Anne Weisberg, *Mass Career Customization: Aligning the Workplace with Today's Nontraditional Workforce* (Boston: Harvard Business School Press, 2007).

66. "About Us," Thrivent Financial Web site, https://www.thrivent.com/aboutus/.

67. Interview with Barbara Foote, vice president, enterprise effectiveness and talent office, Thrivent Financial, by Molly Anderson, June 10, 2009; Jennifer C. Rankin, "One Size Does Not Fit All," *Resource Magazine,* July 2009, 14.

68. Rankin, "One Size Does Not Fit All," 15.

69. Interview with Barbara Foote, June 10, 2009.

70. Interview with Barbara Foote, by Karen McDonald, May 15, 2009.

71. Barb Foote, Andy Liakopoulos, Bill McKinney, "Creating a Career Culture" (presentation for the Association for Strategic Planning, Minneapolis, February 12, 2009).
72. Interview with Barbara Foote, June 10, 2009.

CHAPTER 4

1. Interview with Anne Mulcahy, chairman of Xerox Corporation, by Cathy Benko, July 27, 2009.
2. Robert Half International and CareerBuilder.com, *The Employment Dynamics and Growth Expectations (EDGE) Report* (Menlo Park, CA: Robert Half International, September 2008), http://www.rhi.com/EDGEReport2008.
3. Equal Opportunities Commission, *Enter the Timelords: Transforming Work to Meet the Future* (Manchester, UK: EOC, June 2007), http://www.dhcgroup.co.uk/docs/Transformation_timelords_report[1].pdf.
4. Families and Work Institute, *When Work Works: 2009 Guide to Bold New Ideas for Making Work Work* (New York: Families and Work Institute, August 2009), http://familiesandwork.org/site/research/reports/2009boldideas.pdf.
5. Ibid.
6. Michael Gadd, "More Workers Telecommuting," *Inc.com,* August 28, 2008, http://www.inc.com/news/articles/2008/08/telecommuting.html.
7. Amy Lyman, director of corporate research, Great Places to Work Institute, e-mail to Laura Stokker, July 15, 2009.
8. C. William Day, "Office Space," *American School & University* 81, no. 10 (May 2009), http://asumag.com/Construction/technology/technology-education-office-200905.
9. Don Durfee, "Take My Desk—Please," *CFO Magazine,* October 1, 2006, http://www.cfo.com/article.cfm/7960833?f=search.
10. CoreNet Global Research Center, cited in PeopleCube, "Transforming Individual Workspace into Shared Workspace," http://www.peoplecube.com/products-resource-scheduler-hoteling.htm.
11. Interview with Mark Klender, location strategy leader for comprehensive shared services, Deloitte Consulting LLP, by Cathy Benko, July 7, 2009.
12. Durfee, "Take My Desk—Please."
13. Leigh Stringer, "Reducing Office Space with Alternative Work Strategies," *FacilitiesNet,* November 2008, http://www.facilitiesnet.com/ceilingsfurniturewalls/article/Reducing-Office-Space-with-Alternative-Work-Strategies--10083.
14. Jodi Williams, "Change Management Helps Sprint Nextel Employees Move into New Office Strategy," *FacilitiesNet,* November 2009, http://www.facilitiesnet.com/ceilingsfurniturewalls/article/Change-Management-Helps-Sprint-Nextel-Move-Employees-Into-New-Office-Strategy--11269.
15. Claire Shipman and Katty Kay, *Womenomics* (New York: Harper Collins, 2009), 29.
16. Erin Killian, "National Science Foundation Finds Telework Program Helps Productivity," *Washington Business Journal,* March 11, 2008, http://www.bizjournals.com/washington/stories/2008/03/10/daily19.html?t=printable.
17. Interview with Chris Park, national practice leader, enterprise sustainability, Deloitte Consulting LLP, by Cathy Benko, July 8, 2009.
18. Ibid.
19. Teleworker Exchange Web site, http://www.teleworkexchange.com.

20. Sarah Scalet, "IT Execs from Three Wall Street Companies—Lehman Brothers, Merrill Lynch, and American Express—Look Back on 9/11 and Take Stock of Where They Are Now," *CIO Magazine,* September 1, 2002, http://www.cio.com/article/print/31295.

21. *BT Workstyle Case Study: Flexible Working Provides a Better Work Life Balance* (London: BT, 2006), http://www2.bt.com/static/i/media/pdf/campaigns/consumer_goods/bt%20workstyle_cs.pdf.

22. "Teleworking Increases Productivity and Morale, Saves Money," *Government Technology,* July 6, 2005, http://www.govtech.com/gt/articles/94557.

23. Stanley Kaczmarczyk, "Telework: Breaking New Ground: Successful Telework Programs Feature Active Top-Level Leadership, Clear Policy and Guidelines, Solid Program Support, and Integration in Overall Agency Planning," *Public Manager,* March 22, 2008, http://findarticles.com/p/articles/mi_m0HTO/is_1_37/ai_n27964145/.

24. Ibid.; see also "USPTO Deputy Director Peterlin Testifies at House Committee Hearing on Telework," USPTO press release, November 6, 2007, http://www.uspto.gov/web/offices/com/speeches/07-45.htm.

25. WFD Consulting, *Innovative Workplace Flexibility Options for Hourly Workers* (Washington, DC: Corporate Voices for Working Families, 2009), http://www.cvworkingfamilies.org/publications/2/9.

26. Quoted in Adam Brant, "The Keeper of That Tapping Pen," *New York Times,* March 21, 2009, http://www.nytimes.com/2009/03/22/business/22corner.html.

27. Interview with Matthew Burkley, chief financial officer, Thomson Reuters sales and trading division, by Cathy Benko, August 18, 2009, with follow-up interview on August 29, 2009.

28. Interview with Mike Davis, senior vice president, global human resources, and Kevin Wilde, chief learning officer, General Mills, by Cathy Benko and Laura Stokker, June 15, 2009.

29. Interview with Amy Titus, former global talent development leader, BearingPoint, by Anne Weisberg, July 8, 2009; this case study is based in part on a presentation by Mike Critelli, retired CEO of Pitney Bowes, at the Building Workforce Readiness Through Adult Literacy and Basic Education conference in Washington, D.C., June 18, 2009.

30. Interview with Mike Davis and Kevin Wilde, June 15, 2009.

31. Interview with Tanya Clemons, senior vice president and chief talent officer, Pfizer, by Cathy Benko, June 11, 2009, with follow-up interview by Cathy Benko and Laura Stokker, June 26, 2009.

32. F. Warren McFarlan and Cathy Benko, "Managing a Growth Culture: How CEOs Can Initiate and Monitor a Successful Growth-Project Culture," *Strategy & Leadership* 32, no. 1 (2004): 34–42.

33. Project Management Institute, "Tap into the Amazing Growth of Project Management," pmiteach.org/your-free-downloads/PMI_GAP_Whitepaper_final.pdf.

34. Leslie A. Higham, "Business School Opportunities to Address the Gap in Global Project Management Needs" (presentation at the 2009 ACBSP Annual Conference, San Antonio, TX, June 2009).

35. Arvind Malhotra, "Using Far-Flung Virtual Teams for Managing Knowledge in Global Companies," *UNC Business,* Fall 2004, http://www.kenan-flagler.unc.edu/news/alumnimag/2004fall/global.html.

36. Frank Piller and Ashok Kumar, "Mass Customization: Providing Custom Products and Services with Mass Production Efficiency," *Journal of Financial Transformation,*

http://www.capco.com/files/pdf/66/03_INDUSTRIALIZATION/08_Mass%20customization
%20providing%20custom%20products%20and%20services%20with%20mass%20
production%20efficiency.pdf.

37. Candace Jones, "Careers in Project Networks: The Case of the Film Industry," in *The Boundaryless Career,* eds. Michael B. Arthur and Denise Rousseau (Oxford: Oxford University Press, 1996), 59.

38. Ibid., 65.

39. Interview with Lotte Bailyn, professor of management, MIT, by Molly Anderson, Anne Weisberg, and Laura Stokker, July 15, 2009.

40. David Leonhardt, "Financial Careers Come at a Cost to Families," *New York Times,* May 26, 2009, http://www.nytimes.com/2009/05/27/business/economy/27leonhardt.html.

41. Eurofound, *Functional Flexibility Good for Skills Development* (Dublin: European Working Conditions Observatory, February 26, 2004), http://www.eurofound.europa.eu/ewco/2004/02/NL0402NU03.htm.

42. Terry Desombre, Clare Kelliher, Fraser Macfarlane, and Mustafa Ozbilgin, "Re-Organizing Work Roles in Health Care: Evidence from the Implementation of Functional Flexibility," *British Journal of Management* 17 (2006): 139–151.

43. Interview with Amy Titus, July 8, 2009.

44. Erin Killian, "National Science Foundation Finds Telework Program Helps Productivity."

45. Real Estate Executive Board, *The Productive Workplace, Prioritizing Investments to Enhance Productivity and Reduce Costs* (Washington, DC: Corporate Executive Board, 2005), 57.

46. Lotte Bailyn, "Redesigning Work for Gender Equity and Work-Personal Life Integration" (keynote address delivered at the Community, Work, and Family conference, Utrecht, Netherlands, April 18, 2009, http://web.mit.edu/workplacecenter/docs/keynote.pdf).

47. Ibid.

48. Interview with Tanya Clemons, June 26, 2009.

49. Kim Elsbach, Daniel M. Cable, and Jeffrey Sherman, "How Passive 'Face Time' Affects Perceptions of Employees: Evidence of Spontaneous Trait Inference in Context," research paper 08-08, UC Davis Graduate School of Management, Davis, CA, September 29, 2008, http://ssrn.com/abstract=1295006.

50. WFD Consulting, *Innovative Workplace Flexibility Options for Hourly Workers.*

51. Interview with Lotte Bailyn, July 15, 2009.

52. Interview with George Bouri, national capital and real estate transformation leader, Deloitte Consulting LLP, by Cathy Benko, July 17, 2009.

CHAPTER 5

1. Richard Adler, *Leveraging the Talent-Driven Organization* (Washington, DC: Aspen Institute, January 2010).

2. Robert Hof, interview of Gilbert Cloyd, chief technology officer, P&G, "At P&G, It's '360-Degree Innovation,'" *BusinessWeek.com,* October 11, 2004, http://www.businessweek.com/magazine/content/04_41/b3903463.htm.

3. "Getting Togetherness," *Economist.com,* April 7, 2009, http://www.economist.com/businessfinance/displayStory.cfm?story_id=13435337&CFID=77750615&CFTOKEN=94680929.

4. Patricia Sellers, "P&G: Teaching an Old Dog New Tricks," *Fortune,* May 31, 2004, http://money.cnn.com/magazines/fortune/fortune_archive/2004/05/31/370714/index.htm.

5. *Doctoral Careers: Research & Development,* recruiting brochure, P&G Careers Web site, September 2007, http://www.pg.com/science/Doctoral_Recruiting_Brochure.pdf.

6. Interview with Cynthia Heckmann, chief human capital officer (now retired), and Carol Willett, chief learning officer (now retired), Government Accountability Office, by Cathy Benko and Molly Anderson, July 23, 2009.

7. Jacques Bughin and James Manyika, "How Businesses Are Using Web 2.0: A McKinsey Global Survey," *McKinsey Quarterly,* March 2007, http://www.mckinsey quarterly.com/Marketing/Digital_Marketing/How_businesses_are_using_Web_20_A_McKinsey_Global_Survey_1913.

8. Joi Ito, "Leadership in World of Warcraft," Blog, March 16, 2006, http://joi.ito.com/weblog/2006/03/13/leadership-in-w.html.

9. Martin Hoegl, Katharina Weinkauf, and Hans Georg Gemuenden, "Interteam Coordination, Project Commitment, and Teamwork in Multiteam R&D Projects: A Longitudinal Study," *Organization Science* 15, no. 1 (2004): 38–55.

10. Watson Wyatt, *Using Continuous Engagement to Drive Business Results: 2008/2009 WorkCanada Survey Report* (New York: Watson Wyatt, 2009).

11. Interview with John Hagel III and John Seely Brown by Cathy Benko, Molly Anderson, and Suzanne Kounkel MacGibbon, May 11, 2009, with follow-up interviews by Cathy Benko, July 20 and 21, 2009.

12. Interview with Maryam Alavi, professor, Goizueta Business School, Emory University, by Cathy Benko, Aspen Institute Talent Think Tank, July 20, 2009.

13. Interview with Bob Bertagna, senior managing director and head of industrials at Macquarie Capital, by Cathy Benko, May 29, 2009, and follow-up interview by Cathy Benko, July 16, 2009.

14. Interview with Tanya Clemons, senior vice president and chief talent officer, Pfizer, by Cathy Benko and Laura Stokker, June 26, 2009.

15. Scott Page, *The Difference: How the Power of Diversity Creates Better Groups, Firms, Schools, and Societies* (Princeton, NJ: Princeton University Press, 2007), 157–162.

16. Interview with John Donovan, chief technology officer, AT&T, by Cathy Benko, July 23, 2009, and follow-up interview August 20, 2009.

17. Marc Bien, spokesperson, AT&T, correspondence with Cathy Benko, December 29, 2009.

18. Clive Thompson, "The See-Through CEO," *Wired,* March 2007, http://www.wired.com/wired/archive/15.04/wired40_ceo.html.

19. Jeremiah K. Owyang, *How to Reach Baby Boomers with Social Technologies,* (Cambridge, MA: Forrester Research, January 23, 2009).

20. "Social Networking and Reputational Risk in the Workplace," Deloitte LLP 2009 Ethics & Workplace Survey (New York: Deloitte LLP, 2009), 2.

21. David Carroll, "United Breaks Guitars," July 6, 2009, http://www.youtube.com/watch?v=5YGc4zOqozo&feature=fvw; *The Today Show,* July 19, 2009.

22. "Social Networking and Reputational Risk in the Workplace,"

23. Jennifer Rock, director employee communications, Best Buy, "Company as Wiki—Best Buy," August 27, 2008, http://www.youtube.com/watch?v=H_jhLGxH-m4&feature=player_embedded.

24. Patrick Thibodeau, "Best Buy Getting Results from Social Network," *Computerworld,* March 3, 2009, http://www.computerworld.com/s/article/9128877/ Best_Buy_getting_results_from_social_network_.

25. Charlene Li and Josh Bernoff, *Groundswell: Winning in a World Transformed by Social Technologies* (Boston: Harvard Business Press, 2008), 217–220.

26. Rick Aristotle Munarriz, "Best Buy: Down with Executives?" *Motley Fool,* September 16, 2008, http://www.fool.com/investing/value/2008/09/16/best-buy-down-with-executives.aspx; "Best Buy Taps Prediction Market," *Wall Street Journal,* September 16, 2008, http://online.wsj.com/article/SB122152452811139909.html.

27. "Social Media an Increasingly Important Tool in Keeping Employees Engaged During Tough Economic Times, Survey Finds," Reuters.com, June 9, 2009, http://www.reuters.com/article/pressRelease/idUS107801+09-Jun-2009+ BW20090609.

28. Watson Wyatt, *Using Continuous Engagement to Drive Business Results.*

29. *World of Work* (Wakefield, MA: Randstad, 2008), http://www.us.randstad.com/2008Worldof Work.pdf.

30. Richard Wellins, Paul Bernthal, and Mark Phelps, *Employee Engagement: The Key to Realizing Competitive Advantage* (Pittsburgh: Development Dimensions International, 2005), http://www.ddiworld.com/pdf/ddi_employeeengagement_mg.pdf.

31. Ferda Erdem, Janset Ozen, and Nuray Atsan, "The Relationship Between Trust and Team Performance," *Work Study: A Journal of Productivity Science* 52, no. 6-7 (2003): 337–340.

32. Watson Wyatt, *Weathering the Storm: A Study of Employee Attitudes and Opinions* (New York: Watson Wyatt, 2002), http://www.morganintl.com/June08/SHRM.pdf.

33. Scott Cook, "The Contribution Revolution: Letting Volunteers Build Your Business," *Harvard Business Review* (October 2008): 60–69.

34. Interview with Scott Cook, cofounder and chairman of the Executive Committee, Intuit, by Cathy Benko, Aspen Institute Talent Think Tank, July 20, 2009.

35. Adler, *Leveraging the Talent-Driven Organization.*

36. Interview with Scott Cook, July 20, 2009.

37. Interview with Ben Edwards, publisher and executive vice president, Economist.com, by Cathy Benko, Aspen Institute Talent Think Tank, July 21, 2009.

38. Renee Hopkins Callahan, "Creating a New Kind of Health Care Community," *Forbes,* March 3, 2009, http://www.forbes.com/2009/03/03/patientslikeme-community-database-leadership-clayton-christensen_disruptor_month.html.

39. Interview with Richard Dennison, principal business partner, BT, by Molly Anderson, Suzanne Kounkel MacGibbon, and Laura Stokker, July 23, 2009.

40. Interview with Edith Hunt, COO of human capital management and head of global recruiting, Goldman Sachs; Carol Pledger, talent assessment and performance management, Goldman Sachs University; and Aynesh Johnson, diversity leader, Goldman Sachs, by Cathy Benko and Molly Anderson, July 9, 2009.

41. Interview with Richard Dennison, July 23, 2009.

CHAPTER 6

1. "Cisco Pushes Past Microsoft in Market Value," CBSMarketWatch.com, March 25, 2000, http://www.marketwatch.com/story/cisco-pushes-past-microsoft-in-market-value.

2. Peter Burrows, "Cisco's Comeback," *BusinessWeek,* November 24, 2003, http://www.businessweek.com/magazine/content/03_47/b3859008.htm; Jena McGregor,

"Smart Management for Tough Times," *BusinessWeek*, March 12, 2009, http://www.businessweek.com/magazine/content/09_12/b4124030837359.htm?chan=magazine+channel_game-changing+ideas

3. Ashlee Vance, "Cisco's Net Income Falls but Outlook Improves," *New York Times*, August 5, 2009, http://www.nytimes.com/2009/08/06/technology/companies/06cisco.html?_r=1&scp=2&sq=Cisco&st=cse. See also "Cisco Reports Q1 FY10 Earnings," Cisco press release, November 4, 2009, http://newsroom.cisco.com/dlls/2009/fin_110409.html.

4. "100 Best Companies to Work for 2009," *Fortune*, 2009, http://money.cnn.com/magazines/fortune/bestcompanies/2009/full_list/; "The *DiversityInc* Top 10 Global Diversity Companies List," *DiversityInc*, 2009, http://diversityinc.com/content/1757/article/5862/?The_DiversityInc_Top_10_Global_Diversity_Companies_List; "*Working Mother* 100 Best Companies 2009: Cisco," *Working Mother*, 2009, http://www.workingmother.com/BestCompanies/work-life-balance/2009/08/cisco; "Best Places to Launch a Career 2009," *BusinessWeek*, 2009, http:// bwnt.businessweek.com/interactive_reports/career_launch_2009/.

5. Interview with Brian Schipper, senior vice president of human resources, Cisco, and Susan Monaghan, vice president of employee engagement, Cisco, by Cathy Benko, Thomas Galizia, and Molly Anderson, September 28, 2009.

6. Interview with Randy Pond, executive vice president of operations, systems, and processes, Cisco, by Cathy Benko, Molly Anderson, and Thomas Galizia, July 29, 2009.

7. Burrows, "Cisco's Comeback."

8. Interview with Randy Pond, July 29, 2009.

9. Interview with Brian Schipper and Susan Monaghan, September 28, 2009.

10. Ellen McGirt, "How Cisco's CEO John Chambers Is Turning the Tech Giant Socialist," *Fast Company*, December 2008, http://www.fastcompany.com/magazine/131/revolution-in-san-jose.

11. Ibid.

12. Interview with Don Proctor, senior vice president of software, Cisco, by Cathy Benko, July 17, 2009.

13. McGirt, "How Cisco's CEO John Chambers Is Turning the Tech Giant Socialist."

14. Interview with Brian Schipper and Susan Monaghan, September 28, 2009.

15. Ibid.

16. Peter Burrows, "Cisco's Extreme Ambitions," *BusinessWeek*, November 30, 2009, http://www.businessweek.com/magazine/content/09_48/b4157026785871_page_2.htm.

17. McGregor, "Smart Management for Tough Times."

18. Interview with Brian Schipper and Susan Monaghan, September 28, 2009.

19. McGregor, "Smart Management for Tough Times."

20. Interview with Ana Corrales, vice president, global business operations, Cisco, by Molly Anderson and Thomas Galizia, December 22, 2009.

21. Interview with Randy Pond, July 29, 2009.

22. Mark Landler, "Cisco Chief Calls Productivity the New Engine of Wealth," *New York Times*, January 27, 2004, http://www.nytimes.com/2004/01/27/business/technology-cisco-chief-calls-productivity-new-engine-of-wealth.html?pagewanted=all.

23. Cisco, "Office Design Case Study: How Cisco Designed the Collaborative Connected Workplace Environment," http://www.cisco.com/web/about/ciscoitatwork/business_of_it/connected_workplace_web.html.

24. Ibid.

25. Cisco, "Voice over IP Yields Unexpected Benefits," Case Study, http://www.cisco.com/web/about/ciscoitatwork/trends/tr_2009_01_article012_uc_comm_and_collaboration_benefits.html.

26. "Cisco Study Finds Telecommuting Significantly Increases Employee Productivity, Work-Life Flexibility and Job Satisfaction," Cisco press release, June 26, 2009, http://newsroom.cisco.com/dlls/2009/prod_062609.html.

27. McGirt, "How Cisco's CEO John Chambers Is Turning the Tech Giant Socialist."

28. Marisa Chancellor, "Web 2.0 Collaboration in the Enterprise" (keynote address, N2Y4 NetSquared conference, San Jose, California, May 26, 2009), http://www.netsquared.org/blog/amy-sample-ward/n2y4-marisa-chancellor-cisco-systems-keynote.

29. Interview with Randy Pond, July 29, 2009.

30. "Cisco Study Finds Telecommuting Significantly Increases Employee Productivity, Work-Life Flexibility and Job Satisfaction."

31. Interview with Susan Monaghan, vice president of employee engagement, and Marilyn Nagel, chief diversity officer, both at Cisco, by Cathy Benko, Molly Anderson, Suzanne Kounkel MacGibbon, and Thomas Galizia, May 11, 2009, and follow-up interview by Cathy Benko, Molly Anderson, and Thomas Galizia, August 27, 2009.

32. Lindsey Gerdes, "Why New Grads Love Cisco," *BusinessWeek*, September 3, 2009, http://www.businessweek.com/magazine/content/09_37/b4146038022259.htm?chan=magazine+channel_special+report.

33. Interview with Susan Monaghan and Marilyn Nagel, May 11, 2009.

34. Leah Schnurr, "Dow Gets Shake-Up as GM, Citi Kicked Out of Average," June 1, 2009, Reuters.com, http://www.reuters.com/article/asiaDealsNews/idUSTRE55043Y20090601.

35. As used in this book, "Deloitte" means Deloitte LLP and its subsidiaries. Please see www.deloitte.com/us/about for a detailed description of the legal structure of Deloitte LLP and its subsidiaries. For headcount and revenue information, see "Facts & Figures," https://www.deloitte.com/view/en_US/us/press/Facts-Figures/ index.htm.

36. Interview with Barry Salzberg, CEO, Deloitte LLP, by Cathy Benko and Molly Anderson, August 12, 2009.

37. Workforce statistics from internal HR analytics, 2005; Beatrice Sanders, *The Supply of Accounting Graduates and the Demand for Public Accounting Recruits—2005, for Academic Year 2003–2004* (New York: AICPA, 2005), 9, http://ceae.aicpa.org/NR/rdonlyres/11715FC6-F0A7-4AD6-8D28-6285CBE77315/0/Supply_DemandReport_2005.pdf.

38. Ashley Goodall and Jeff Summer, *The Talent Landscape* (New York: Deloitte internal white paper, May 2006), 12.

39. Deloitte internal HR analysis of exit interview data from external vendor, 2005–2006.

40. Interview with Bill Freda, managing partner of clients and markets, Deloitte LLP, by Cathy Benko, October 21, 2009.

41. Diane Brady and Jena McGregor, "What Works in Women's Networks," *BusinessWeek*, June 18, 2007, http://www.businessweek.com/magazine/content/07_25/b4039069.htm.

42. "Deloitte Continues to Strengthen Its Commitment to Diversity and Inclusion with New Program for Black/African-American Accountants," Deloitte press release, June 30, 2005, http://www.csrwire.com/press/press_release/21891-Deloitte-Continues-To-Strengthen-Its-Commitment-To-Diversity-Inclusion-With-New-Program-For-Black-African-American-Accountants.

43. "How Coaching Helps a 'Big Four' Accounting Firm Retain Staff," *HR Focus*, January 3, 2006, https://www.cpp.com/Pdfs/deloitte.pdf; "A Living, Breathing People Strategy," *Training & Development*, October 2007, http://findarticles.com/p/articles/mi_m4467/is_200710/ai_n21297010/.

44. Deloitte internal exit interview data.

45. Laura Fitzpatrick, "We're Getting Off the Ladder," *Time*, May 25, 2009.

46. Deloitte internal employee attitude surveys administered at regular intervals during the MCC tool implementation, 2007–2009.

47. Deloitte internal statistics from HR analytics retention reports, 2006–2008.

48. Interview with Joe Echevarria, U.S. managing partner, operations, Deloitte LLP, by Cathy Benko, August 25, 2009.

49. Interviews and correspondence with Jia Li Moore, senior manager, Deloitte Consulting LLP; Mike Ranken, manager, Deloitte & Touche LLP; and Mike Jacobson, senior associate, Deloitte Financial Advisory Services LLP; by Molly Anderson, Anne Weisberg, and Megan Farrell, October–November, 2008.

50. Deloitte internal analysis of employees' MCC profiles, 2007–2009.

51. Interview with Jim Jaeger, managing partner, talent, Deloitte LLP, by Cathy Benko, September 1, 2009.

52. Deloitte internal employee attitude surveys.

53. Interview with Bill Pelster, chief learning officer, Deloitte LLP, by Molly Anderson, September 3, 2009.

54. Ibid.

55. Interview with Barry Salzberg, August 12, 2009.

56. Deloitte Research, *Why Change Now? Preparing for the Workplace of Tomorrow* (New York: Deloitte Development LLC, 2009), 9.

57. Deloitte internal data from Innovation Quest system, 2009.

58. Interview with John Levis, chief strategy officer, Deloitte LLP, by Cathy Benko and Molly Anderson, September 2, 2009.

59. Interview with Sharon Allen, chairman of the board, Deloitte LLP, by Cathy Benko, September 14, 2009.

60. Deloitte internal communication regarding D Street implementation.

61. Interview with Chet Wood, chief executive officer, Deloitte Tax LLP, by Cathy Benko, September 2, 2009.

62. Deloitte internal statistics from D Street system, January 2009.

63. Mary Brandel, "The New Employee Connection: Social Networking Behind the Firewall," *ComputerWorld*, August 11, 2008, http://www.computerworld.com/s/article/322857/The_new_employee_connection_Social_networking_behind_the_firewall?taxonomyID=16&pageNumber=1.

64. *The Talent Dashboard: An Executive Overview of Talent Performance* (New York: Deloitte internal document, May 30, 2009), and workforce planning and tracking management report, May 2008.

65. Ibid.; Deloitte internal documents with results of annual talent survey conducted by external vendor, 2005–2009.

66. "Best Places to Launch a Career 2009," *BusinessWeek*, 2009, http://bwnt. businessweek.com/interactive_reports/career_launch_2009/; "100 Best Companies to Work for 2009," *Fortune*, 2009, http://money.cnn.com/magazines/fortune/ bestcompanies/2009/full_list/; "The 9th Annual 2009 *DiversityInc* Top 50 Companies for Diversity," *DiversityInc*, 2009, http://www.diversityinc.com/public/department289. cfm; "*Working Mother* 100 Best Companies 2009," *Working Mother*, September 2009, http://www.workingmother.com/BestCompanies/ node/1671/list?page=1.

67. "Training Top 10 Hall of Fame 2009," *Training*, February 23, 2008, http:// www.trainingmag.com/msg/content_display/publications/e3id4a71ae8a1475303c 59a3586ab4acf37.

68. Brad Harrington and Jamie G. Ladge, "Got Talent? It Isn't Hard to Find," in *The Shriver Report: A Woman's Nation Changes Everything* (Washington, DC: Center for American Progress, 2009), http://www.awomansnation.com/business.php.

69. "Catalyst Recognizes Initiatives at Campbell Soup Company, Deloitte, Royal Bank of Canada, and Telstra with the 2010 Catalyst Award," Catalyst press release, January 21, 2010, http://www.catalyst.org/press-release/159/catalyst-recognizes-initiatives-at-campbell-soup-company-deloitte-royal-bank-of-canada-and-telstra-with-the-2010-catalyst-award.

70. Thomson Reuters total revenues are $13.4 billion, according to the 2008 Thomson Reuters Annual Review.

71. Correspondence between Sharon Rowlands, former president and chief executive officer, Thomson Financial, and Cathy Benko and Molly Anderson, September15, 2009.

72. Interview with David Turner, executive vice president and current chief financial officer, Thomson Reuters Markets, by Cathy Benko and Molly Anderson, September 29, 2009.

73. "Thomson Reuters Upbeat on Asian Region," *The Hindu*, April 18, 2008, http://www.thehindu.com/2008/04/18/stories/2008041855431700.htm.

74. Interview with David Turner, September 29, 2009.

75. Interview with Anna Patruno, global head of financial business operations, Thomson Reuters Markets, by Molly Anderson, October 9, 2009.

76. Ibid.

77. Camilla Berens, "How Reuters Uses Technology and State-of-the-Art Workplaces to Reach Peak Efficiency," *FMWorld*, February 21, 2008, http://74.125.155. 132/search?q=cache:tc95eu-k87AJ:www.fmlink.com/ProfResources/Magazines/ article.cgi%3FFM%2520World:fmworld022408.html+reuters+facility+management &cd=11&hl=en&ct=clnk&gl=us.

78. Thomson Reuters 2008 Employee Survey. The Thomson Reuters flexibility approval rating of 80 percent was compared against a group of high-performing companies worldwide comprising approximately 140,000 employee surveys in the same time frame by Towers Perrin/ISR. The average flexibility approval rating for these companies was 75 percent.

79. Interview with David Turner, September 29, 2009.

80. Interview with Anna Patruno, October 9, 2009.

81. Interview with Matthew Burkley, chief financial officer, Thomson Reuters Sales and Trading Division, by Cathy Benko, August 26, 2009, and by Molly Anderson, September 9, 2009, and correspondence August and September, 2009.

82. Interview with David Turner, September 29, 2009.

83. Interview with Anna Patruno, October 9, 2009.

84. Interview with David Turner, September 29, 2009.

85. Interview with Anna Patruno, October 9, 2009.

86. Employee engagement and thirteen different organizational attributes are measured through a survey of all Thomson Reuters employees, which is conducted by Towers Perrin/ISR using its Engagement Index.

87. Ibid.

88. Interview with Anna Patruno, October 9, 2009.

89. 2006 ThomsonPlus and Q2 Financial Review including FinancePlus.

90. Interview with David Turner, September 29, 2009.

91. Ibid.

CHAPTER 7

1. Interview with Robyn Denholm, chief financial officer, Juniper Networks, by Cathy Benko, May 6, 2009, and follow-up by Cathy Benko, June 15, 2009.

2. E-mail from Pattie Sellers, editor at large, *Fortune,* to Cathy Benko, August 6, 2009.

3. Interview with Matthew Burkley, chief financial officer, Thomson Reuters Sales and Trading division, by Cathy Benko, August 26, 2009, and follow-up by Molly Anderson, September 9, 2009.

4. Interview with Mike Davis, senior vice president, global human resources, and Kevin Wilde, chief learning officer, General Mills, by Cathy Benko and Laura Stokker, June 15, 2009.

5. Interview with Robyn Denholm, May 6, 2009, and June 15, 2009.

6. Interview with Harry Max, principal, Clarify LLC, by Molly Anderson and Karen Crandall, February, 12, 2010 and by Karen Crandall, July 6, 2009.

7. Ibid.

8. Interview with Anne Mulcahy, chairman, Xerox Corporation, by Cathy Benko, July 27, 2009.

9. Clare Kaufman, "Seven Secrets for Building Marketable Skills," DegreesAnd-Training.com, http://encarta.degreesandtraining.com/articles.jsp?article=featured_seven_secrets_for_building_marketable_skills.

10. *Canadians Say More Training Vital to Remain Competitive in Job Market* (Troy, MI: Kelly Global Workforce Index, April 29, 2009), http://www.kellyservices.ca/res/content/ca/services/en/docs/kgwi-canada_sustainability_of_talent_eng_apr-09.pdf.

11. Interview with John DiMare, partner, Crown Advisors, by Karen Crandall, July 1, 2009.

12. Interview with E. Gordon Gee, president, The Ohio State University, by Cathy Benko and Suzanne Kounkel MacGibbon, September 18, 2009.

13. John Phillip Jones, *How to Use Advertising to Build Strong Brands* (Thousand Oaks, CA: Sage Publications, 1999), 161.

14. Tom Peters, "The Brand Called You," *Fast Company,* August 1997, http://www.fastcompany.com/magazine/10/brandyou.html.

15. Interview with Richard Dennison, principal business partner, BT, by Molly Anderson, Suzanne Kounkel MacGibbon, and Laura Stokker, July 23, 2009.

16. Beth Kowitt, "The Best Advice I Ever Got: Be Willing to Do It Yourself," *Fortune,* March 30, 2009.

17. Peters, "The Brand Called You."

18. Erin Burt, "Ten Job Hunting Myths," *Washington Post,* February 22, 2008, http://www.washingtonpost.com/wp-dyn/content/article/2008/02/22/AR2008022201109_ pf.html.

19. Mary Madden et al., *Digital Footprints: Online Identity Management and Search in the Age of Transparency* (Washington, DC: Pew Internet and American Life Project, December 14, 2007), http://pewinternet.org/Reports/2007/Digital-Footprints.aspx.

20. "Nearly Half of Employers Have Caught a Lie on a Resume, CareerBuilder.com Survey Shows," CareerBuilder.com, July 30, 2008, http://www.careerbuilder.com/share/aboutus/pressreleasesdetail.aspx?id=pr448&sd=7/30/2008&ed=7/30/2099.

21. Deborah Ben-Canaan and Martha Fay Africa, "Keep Your Resume Honest," Law.com, September 22, 2009, http://www.law.com/jsp/law/careercenter/lawArticle CareerCenter.jsp?id=1202433956898.

22. William Arruda and Kirsten Dixson, *Career Distinction: Stand Out by Building Your Brand* (Hoboken, NJ: John Wiley & Sons, 2007), 4.

23. Jim Friedel, former senior vice president, Northwest Airlines, correspondence with Molly Anderson and Karen Crandall, September 10, 2009, and interview with Karen Crandall, June 26, 2009.

24. Interview with Carol Carpenter, general manager, consumer and small business, TrendMicro, by Karen Crandall, June 26, 2009, and follow-up by Cathy Benko, September 11, 2009.

25. John Hagel III, John Seely Brown, and Lang Davison, *Measuring the Forces of Long-Term Change: The 2009 Shift Index* (San Jose, CA: Deloitte Center for the Edge, 2009), http://www.deloitte.com/assets/Dcom-UnitedStates/Local%20Assets/Documents/us_tmt_ce_ShiftIndex_072109ecm.pdf.

26. Douglas Elmendorf, Gregory Mankiw, and Lawrence H. Summers, eds., *Brookings Papers on Economic Activity* (Washington, DC: Brookings Institution Press, Spring 2008).

INDEX

ABOUT THE AUTHORS

Cathy Benko is Vice Chairman and Chief Talent Officer at Deloitte LLP, the largest professional services firm in the United States. In this role, Cathy sets the strategy and leads the delivery of Deloitte's signature talent experience to a highly skilled and diverse workforce. She is a leading authority on talent strategies and transformational change to achieve exceptional results. Previously, she served as Deloitte Consulting LLP's global e-business leader and subsequently led the high-technology industry sector as well as the organization's award-winning Women's Initiative.

Cathy has been named a "Frontline Leader" by *Consulting* magazine and is the recipient of its inaugural Leadership Achievement Award for Women Leaders. She also has been cited by a number of prestigious organizations, including Women in Technology International (WITI) and the *San Francisco Business Times*, which has named her one of the "Most Influential Women in the Bay Area" for eight consecutive years.

Cathy is coauthor of the bestseller *Mass Career Customization: Aligning the Workplace with Today's Nontraditional Workforce* (Harvard Business Press, 2007) and *Connecting the Dots: Aligning Projects with Objectives in Unpredictable Times* (Harvard Business Press, 2003). Her byline and other contributed insights have appeared in such publications as the *New York Times*, *Ivey Business Journal*, *Strategy + Leadership*, *BusinessWeek*, the *Wall Street Journal*, *Time*, *Workforce Management*, and other national media outlets, including major television business and news channels.

Cathy serves on Deloitte LLP's executive committee and global talent council. She is a member of *Consulting Magazine*'s advisory board and the Western Advisory Council for Catalyst and was recently a judge for *Harvard Business Review*'s McKinsey Awards. Cathy earned her MBA from Harvard Business School and lives in Northern California with her husband and two children.

Molly Anderson is Director of Talent for Deloitte Services LP, specializing in innovative strategies to engage today's increasingly diverse, knowledge-based workforce. She designed and led the implementation of Mass Career Customization across Deloitte's forty-three-thousand-person organization, significantly increasing career–life satisfaction, retention, and engagement.

Prior to her current role, Molly directed Deloitte's highly acclaimed Women's Initiative, leading programs to advance women through leadership development, innovation, community building, and marketplace eminence.

Molly is an authority on organizational effectiveness, human resources strategy, and learning and development. She has extensive experience implementing transformational change in large organizations through the integration of processes, people, and technology. Her expertise spans a range of industries and disciplines including health care, higher education, mergers and acquisitions, and customer service.

Molly is a frequent speaker on these topics in forums for the Conference Board, the Professional BusinessWomen of California,

Stanford University, the University of California, and corporate leadership groups in a variety of industries.

Molly earned her MBA from Stanford University and her undergraduate degree from Harvard University. She lives with her husband and two children in Northern California.